How to Write Compelling Stories from Family History

ANNETTE GENDLER

Published by Nana's Books

Interior Book Design by Inspire Books
Cover Design by Dylan Wickstrom
Illustrations by Wei Lu

ISBN: 978-1-7340652-0-6

Printed in the United States

Contents

If you don't remember your past, you will not be able to adequately assess your present. If you don't remember where you came from, you will never be able to judge where you have arrived at.

—Rabbi Shlomo Riskin quoting the Maharal of Prague in "Torah Lights," April 18, 2016

Dear Reader

T his book is meant to help you tackle the often overwhelming project of "doing something" with your family history: the stories you grew up with that no one wrote down (or maybe someone did), the piles of family documents, the boxes of letters and photos, a heap of genealogical research, or a relative's handwritten memories. It could even be the history of another family you care about.

This book will focus on how to shape family history into compelling stories.

It will not teach you how to write memoir per se, but show you how to write a particular type of memoir that captures one or more interesting stories from your family's history. We humans have always transmitted our history, our learnings, and our culture from one generation to the next through storytelling. Stories give meaning to traditions.

I'll introduce you to different ways of shaping family history into compelling stories, based on my own experience writing my memoir *Jumping Over Shadows*. I will also share the experiences of some of my students, in particular those at StoryStudio Chicago, where I have been privileged to shepherd several family stories to fruition. This book includes lots of reading examples because we learn best by seeing how someone else did what we are trying to do. Examples can also serve as models for you to emulate.

I wish you all the best in tackling the project of shaping your family history into compelling stories, and I hope this book will help you along the way.

Annette

Why Family History Matters

O ur family shapes us. It is the nucleus of life. The way we were brought up—and in particular the people who raised us, their habits and foibles, their history—contributed (and still does!) to who we are.

Understanding what shaped us helps us understand who we are.

This understanding applies not only to our immediate family, i.e., mom, dad, and our siblings, stepparents and step-siblings, but also to our grandparents, great-grandparents, aunts and uncles. Who they were shaped our parents—and thus shaped us.

Postmemory: the phenomenon of inheriting our ancestors' memories

In order to understand who our parents, our grandparents, our ancestors were, we need to tell their stories, and that involves their memories. What people remember is already a natural filter of what is interesting about their lives. In her seminal work, *The Generation of Postmemory*, Marianne

Hirsch examines whether we can remember other people's memories. I agree with her that we can. Indeed, other people's memories have a profound effect on us, particularly those of traumatic events.

In his book, *It Didn't Start With You*, Mark Wolynn asserts that inherited family trauma shapes who we are and often messes up our lives until we figure out where the disturbance is coming from. Wolynn presents different processes on how to end the cycle, but before we can even begin to address the effect of trauma, we need to know what it is. That's where storytelling comes in. We need to know our ancestors' stories; we need to know what they suffered, what they lost, what they yearned for and never realized—and also, of course, what they succeeded at and what made them happy.

Those are the stories, the memories, that shaped who we are.

This does not necessarily mean that a particular traumatic event needs to be retold in minute detail, particularly if this proves too unsettling for those who suffered it. Rather, broad brushstrokes of what happened might suffice to acknowledge the trauma and give the pain and/or loss its due. A summary can explain the effect it had and how it framed the lives of those affected going forward. We might not have to unpack the details of a deportation, for example, but if we know that a certain mug is "holy" to Grandma because it is the only piece that survived that event, then we understand its significance. We can capture the story of that trauma by telling the story of that mug.

Trauma is not the only history worth telling.

While trauma is the most forceful of legacies in terms of having a profound impact on subsequent generations, it is not the only thing that matters. It is not as if without trauma, there wouldn't be stories to tell. Quite the contrary.

Nancy Julien Kopp's story of her parents' elopement (see "The Secret" in the Readings section, page 123) is a great example of a memoir that captures a happy event that had a profound impact on the next generation. Without her parents' gumption to get married despite the objection of her mother's family, Nancy would not be around.

On the other hand, is all that happens to us worth telling, worth investing the time to write as memoir? Definitely not. That makes for a lot of boring autobiography. The events that are worth telling do not have to involve high drama—as in death, illness, divorce, or some other traumatic event.

Rather, the events that are worth telling are those that were transformative.

The main character needs to have faced a challenge, to have learned something, and to have been changed by dealing with it. That challenge can be as mundane as moving to a new city or giving up a beloved car. Anything that changed the main character, that gave him an insight he didn't have before, is worth a story. In terms of family history, whatever is felt in the next generation is worth a story.

One rather mundane but happy example from my own life is the story of "The Tractor." I have warm memories of spending time with my American grandfather working with his tractor, so when my husband and I bought our own country property, it was a natural thing for me to buy a tractor.

Then there are the stories no one told or took the time to write down. Just recently, an orthopedic surgeon asked me whether there was a history of hip problems in my family. First, I said no because neither my mother nor my father suffered from hip problems, but then I remembered that my grandmother had two hip replacements in her seventies.

"Are you built like her?" the surgeon asked.

Come to think of it, I am! I have my grandmother's build, so it stands to reason that she might have suffered the same pain I was suffering from now. I wish I could call her and ask how long she suffered pain in her hips, and what in particular set it off. I wish she had left at least a diary for me to consult to see how she dealt with the pain. In that way, I could have learned from her pain.

Alas, she did not do that. While I do have lots of letters from her, she didn't write about her hip pain to her teenage and, later, young adult granddaughter. Fortunately, at least I knew her well, so I now have a likely explanation for my own predicament. In the future, genetics might trace all those bodily inheritances for us. However, our genes won't tell us the related stories, and they won't tell us how a particular ancestor lived with the same genes we now have.

Only a story can help us learn how to live.

All those traits we inherited shape who we are: an uncle's scatterbrain or our mother's love for gardening, a father's bad vision or a great-grandfather's skill in metalworking. Knowing where those traits came from, and who the people we inherited them from really were, gives us a sense of belonging.

Not only does family history help us understand ourselves better; it also gives us the connection we crave.

We humans want to know where we come from and where we belong—not just in a physical sense, but in terms of those who came before us.

The more stories of the past we can capture, the better.

All this makes for a lot of material. Where do we find the most compelling stories?

Prompt:

Write about a family resemblance. Do you have your mother's feet? Does your nephew have your mother's eyes? Or does your uncle have the same hands as your grandfather? Describe them and write about what you feel when you see those hands or think of them.

A Word on Genre

B efore we dive into discussing how to shape family history into compelling stories, let's talk about genre. Memoir and historical fiction are generally the best ways to write stories based on family history.

I am partial to memoir because I believe your family will want to know what really happened, rather than being presented with a novel that leaves them puzzling over what is true and what isn't. That being said, historical fiction has its place and is wildly popular. Make your decision on what genre to write in based on the material you have. If you have enough material, write a memoir, which can be short or book length. If the facts are too scant and you have to make stuff up to create a story that works, write historical fiction, i.e., either a novel (book length) or a short story.

In our times of reality TV, people seem to crave true stories. Memoir has thus become the genre du jour. It is such a buzzword that it gets slapped on to personal stories, whether applicable or not.

A memoir is a true story of the past.

It relies on memory (hence the name) and seeks to find the meaning of that memory. It is also a story that the reader will assume is true.

As soon as you start making something up, you're moving into the realm of fiction.

This is totally fine; just don't put the memoir label on it, or you will get into trouble.

Labels are important because they manage reader expectations.

Hence all the brouhaha when a memoirist is found to have made up parts of his story. Readers expect memoirs to be true, and there is hell to pay if they are not. See the scandals over James Frey's *A Million Little Pieces*, Greg Mortenson's *Three Cups of Tea*, or, even worse, the entirely fabricated Holocaust memoir *Fragments* by Binjamin Wilkomirski.

Truth in memoir is a big topic, and much has been written about it. Being truthful, however, does not mean you have to be literal. When you're writing about an event with grandma, and you say she was wearing her green dress that day, was she indeed wearing a green dress? Maybe you remember and she was indeed. If you don't remember, and you want to describe her dress because the way she dressed says something about what kind of person she was, then put her in one of the dresses you remember she used to wear. It is truthful to who she was, even if she wasn't wearing that particular dress on that particular day. If you're worried about fudging here, you can let the reader in on it by saying, "She might have worn the green dress with the polka dots, but I don't remember." Or if it's a scene you weren't present for, you can speculate: "She might have been wearing her signature green polka dot dress." As long as you're not putting her in a dress she never wore, you're OK.

When a new round of my introductory memoir class convenes at StoryStudio Chicago, I devote the first class to defining memoir. I usually ask students about their favorite memoirs. Once, a student mentioned that she found some memoirs boring.

"Can you give an example?" I asked.

"Well, for instance, Bill Clinton's."

Aha! I sighed with relief because Bill Clinton's 1056-page *My Life* is not a memoir. It's an autobiography. In all fairness, Bill Clinton's editors didn't put "a memoir" on the cover; my student had just thought of it that way. Publishers, it seems, are more cautious about putting the memoir label on the cover. For instance, Katharine Graham's *Personal History* is referred to as memoir on the back cover, whereas on the front, the *New York Times* is quoted: "An extraordinary autobiography . . . touching . . . winning . . . inspiring." This happens often: Autobiography and memoir are used interchangeably.

So what's the difference between autobiography and memoir?

And why should we care? Both are written by the person whose life is being narrated, right? Yes, but autobiography is a chronological account of that life, from birth to a later stage in life. Autobiography is concerned with recounting what happened, with setting the record straight, and with giving a behind-the-scenes glimpse into the life of a usually famous person.

In contrast to memoir, autobiography is less concerned with introspection.

A good memoir is not an accumulation of anecdotes, however entertaining they may be. Rather, it is an inquiry into what those anecdotes mean to the narrator. A memoir does not comprise a whole life; rather, it examines a particular phase in a life. Childhood memoirs are a great example, such as Mary Karr's *The Liars' Club*, Tobias Wolff's *This Boy's Life*, or Frank McCourt's *Angela's Ashes*.

An autobiography is expected to tell everything; in contrast, a memoir tells something, namely whatever can be shared about the chosen topic. This is one reason why memoir lends itself well to writing stories from family history: You often don't know all the details, or maybe you aren't free to write about everything.

Memoir lets you be selective. It lets you pick the relevant stories.

You can write only one autobiography of your life, but you can write many memoirs. Mary Karr is a great example. While *The Liars' Club* recounts the story of her childhood in a dismal Texas oil town and a wildly dysfunctional family, her next memoir *Cherry* is about her promiscuous adolescence, and her most recent *Lit* tells the story of her recovery from alcoholism and finding solace in the Catholic faith. Whereas Mary Karr's memoirs are circumscribed by time, Eileen Simpson's, for example, explore different topics: *Orphans* (losing her parents early in life), *Reversals: A Personal Account of Victory over Dyslexia*, and *Poets in Their Youth* (her tumultuous early marriage to poet John Berryman).

Memoir captures what it is like to live in a particular time and to grapple with, and hopefully overcome, its particular struggles.

This is also why memoir lends itself so well to shaping family history into compelling stories.

Prompt:

Write about one of the homes you grew up in. Include details that bring that time period to life, such as TV shows, books, games, décor, music, food, etc.

How to Find Interesting Stories

Genealogy helps us figure out where our ancestors came from, but it doesn't necessarily make for good stories. You don't want to be the boring aunt at the Thanksgiving table who goes on and on about so-and-so who married so-and-so and emigrated from Poland. You want to find the interesting stories, the ones worth capturing and passing on.

A note of caution: As soon as you find yourself in an "and then this happened, and then that happened" mode, you're boring. Stop and figure out whether this story is actually interesting to those around you. Ask yourself: Why should this story matter to them? What part of it affects them?

Look for where the past affects the present.

That's where the interest lies. Perhaps you still cook grandma's pierogi and you know she got that recipe from the girl so-and-so married? Now that's interesting because it still matters; those pierogies are still on the table.

Your great-aunt's diary of living in a small cabin in the Indiana countryside as a young woman might give an interesting glimpse into daily life in the 1890s, but it does not necessarily make for a good story. You might want to comb through that diary, however, to see if she ever commented on the family feud that caused one uncle to shoot his son and then kill himself. That's your door into her material: you're hunting for something specific to round out another family story that still reverberates through the generations. This example comes from Rebecca McClanahan's beautiful family memoir *The Tribal Knot*, based mainly on old letters.

Or maybe you still have a pail your great-aunt used to have? Then tell the story of that pail (which gives you the necessary focus), what she did with it in that cabin life of hers (which creates her as a character), and why you cherish it (why it still matters in the present).

That's the connection between past and present, and that's what's interesting.

Prompt:

Make a list of items you still own, and perhaps use, that belonged to a loved one.

How Not to Be Boring

✏

How do you find the stories worth telling from the heap of family history? Let's start with an example: Please read "He Can Walk Because of Me" in the Readings Section, page 119.

As you read, ask yourself:

- What is interesting about this story?

- How is it structured?

- What is your reaction as a reader?

Now let's look at this more closely. First of all, the title is enticing; it got me to click on it when this blog post appeared in my inbox. However, the juicy part, the part that matters and the reason I clicked on this story, doesn't appear until the fourth paragraph. We have to read through where this family hailed from, who married whom, and where they lived. In addition, we are bombarded with lots of names that are easily confusing. Who is who, and whom should we as readers care about? Not until the fourth paragraph are any of the people portrayed in such a way that we would care about them.

How would it read if the story began with "He can walk because of me," then moved on to tell the story of how this father advocated for his son when the doctors were giving up on him? The very sentence "He can walk because of me" is where the past affects the present, and why that story is relevant and compelling.

This small snippet of the father's life, when he makes sure his son gets braces on his legs and feet despite all odds, shows the reader what kind of person this father was. He becomes a character, not just a person about whom we learn biographical information. Furthermore, his action, namely advocating for his child, is a lesson in parenting. It gives the reader something to relate to, something to learn from. A reader's situation might be completely different, yet having parents who advocate for their child is a universal thing (or should be!).

Prompt:

Write about a time when your parent(s) advocated for you. If they didn't, reflect on why not.

What's a Story?

S tory is the key to not boring your readers. We all think we know what a story is, right? In order to write one, however, we have to look at its components:

- A specific time

- A specific place

- Character(s) - usually at least one person, but sometimes an inanimate object like a house or the weather can also be a character

- Inciting incident - why are we telling this story?

- Action - the characters need to be doing something

- Change - the characters need to come out differently from the story than they entered

Much has been written about how to write a story (I recommend *Story* by Robert McKee). Since this is not the focus of this book, I am just presenting you with a simple approach to help you look for the stories in your family history. Taking the example of the "He Can Walk Because of Me" blog post on page 119, we can easily sift out the story:

- A specific time - when Walter was born (late 1940s - exact date would be good here)

- A specific place - New Brighton, Pennsylvania

- Character(s) - the father Thomas, the child Walter, at least one doctor who is not named (here is where more research into the story would be appropriate to find out where this happened, who the doctor was, etc.)

- Inciting incident - A child is born deformed and his father is told he can't be helped.

- Action - The father insists that his child be put into braces even though the doctor says it's hopeless.

- Change - Because of the father's insistence on treatment, his son can walk now.

From this list, we can already tell that this could grow into a short memoir with several scenes. The parents finding out about their child's disability could be the first scene. The father deciding what to do could be another, with mainly internal dialogue. Then there could be the showdown with the doctors and another scene with the child toddling around in his braces and the father realizing that his treatment might work. Or there could be a letdown, a disappointment in the middle of the story, when it looks like the treatment might not work, and eventually it does. The last scene could be Walter as an able-bodied adult who regularly visits his elderly father. Somewhere in there, we'd have the seminal line, "He can walk because of me."

Show, don't tell.

This is old advice, and one you will come across in any writing book worth its money. "Show, don't tell" is key to telling stories, but how is it actually achieved in terms of text? A story will consist of scenes and exposition.

> Scene = Show
> Exposition = Tell

"He Can Walk Because of Me" is told. It does not contain a single scene, even though there easily could be one. Only a scene will draw the reader into the space of the story.

So what is a scene?

Think of going to the theater and seeing a play. What you see on the stage is a scene. In fact, drama is all scene. Movies are also largely done in scenes, but, unlike a play, they can also use a bird's-eye view and move around in time more easily. In movie terms, a play is the close-up.

The elements of a scene:

- A specific time

- A specific place

- Actors - Ideally, they will be characters, i.e., fully fledged personalities, but some scenes do work with "cardboard" characters.

- Action - Something happens between the characters, even if they are just talking.

- Forward movement - The action has to move the story forward, and the characters have to end up somewhere other than where they started.

Characters

In any family story, the people will be the most important component, so creating them as characters, as multi-faceted personalities, is crucial. It can be particularly challenging to see someone who has a defined role in your life (such as your grandmother, for example) in a different light. Ask yourself: Who was she as a young girl? Young woman? What challenges did she face? How did she grow up? Who was she as a wife, a sister, a daughter?

While it is hard to see who the people in your family are outside of their familial role, this can also be a rewarding exercise. It will give you a new perspective, especially regarding a difficult person.

As an example, my great-aunt Resi was always seen as the villain in my family. She divorced her Jewish husband, and she was willing to do just about anything to save her children, who were classified as half-Jews by the Nazis and faced increasing discrimination. My grandparents saw her as ruthless and a person without principles, and my grandfather spent a good part of writing his memoirs on trying to understand who she became under Nazi rule. When I first started to workshop my manuscript that featured Resi as one of the main characters, readers felt she was a hero. After all, she managed to save her children, and they were sympathetic to her plight. Because I had grown up with my grandparents' view of her, it took me a while to grant that this was a valid interpretation, but I cherish the fact that thanks to writing her story, I have come to a more nuanced understanding of my family's past.

To create someone as a character, it can be helpful to create a character sketch to see what really brings a person to life. Consider:

- Mannerisms

- Movement

- Habits

- Sayings

- Typical clothing

- Scent

- Hobbies

There are some excellent literary examples, where the author uses one particular trait to characterize a person or a family:

- **Movement**: By describing how Nettie, one of the main characters in her memoir *Fierce Attachments*, walks down the street, Vivian Gornick does an amazing job of characterizing her: "Her walk was slow and deliberate. She moved first one haunch, then the other, making her hips sway. Everyone knew this woman was going nowhere, that she was walking to walk, walking to feel the effect she had on the street. Her walk insisted on the flesh beneath the clothes" (page 98).

- **Scent:** Mary Karr is a master at utilizing smell in her prose. One striking example is the description of her grandmother in *The Liars' Club*: "Once we were in her room, she closed the door and posted herself, wheelchair and all, right in front of it. Let me take a minute to tell you about the smell in that room. It stank of snake, specifically water moccasin. If you are walking in waders through a marsh, say, on a warm winter morning, […] you can smell a moccasin slithering alongside you long before you see it. It has an odor like something dead just before the rot sets in and the worms in its belly skin get it to jiggling around unnaturally" (page 76).

- **Sayings**: *The Things We Used to Say* by Natalia Ginzburg is an entire book devoted to resurrecting a family's "the way we were" by capturing their habitual sayings: "As soon as someone died my father immediately added the word 'poor' to their name and he got angry with my mother because she didn't do the same. This custom of calling people 'poor' was taken very seriously in my father's family; my grandmother, speaking of a dead sister of hers, would invariably say, 'Regina, poor soul,' and never referred to her in any other way" (page 47).

Prompt:

Write about one of your family's sayings. My grandmother/mother/father/uncle used to say, "_____."

Start Small

Life is big. Family history is big. Thus we tend to think of any writing based on family history as a big project—a book project. However, writing a book is a daunting task. Therefore, quite often, capturing stories from family history is never attempted, even though we all have stories to tell.

There is, however, another way: Start small.

Focus on learning how to write one short family story.

A memoir does not have to be a book.

Regarding shorter pieces, I am often asked:

What's the difference between a personal essay and a memoir?

While a personal essay might bring in some memories, it tends to be a story of the present, in which you relate an insight, a realization, an epiphany. A memoir, on the other hand, is a story of the past, even if it is the recent past. It can be short, but it relies on memory and aims to find the meaning of that memory. That's the difference.

You are more likely to find success by going small, by distilling one particular event into a short memoir. Start with whatever story you find most interesting.

Having taught memoir writing for more than ten years, I know that crafting a story from real life is best learned by focusing on one event.

Thankfully, one well-crafted scene can capture more of the mosaic of life than 25 pages of exposition.

Furthermore, by going small, you avoid the structural challenges of a larger work. And if you so desire, the chances of having a short piece published are much higher.

Completing this one story will not only give you the satisfaction of actually "having done something with" a family story, it will also teach you a lot about how to tell and write this kind of story. If you're so inclined, try to get it published. There are so many online publications out there these days, you might just be able to find one that is interested in your topic.

A completed story also gives you something to work with. It sets you on your path. Write another one, then another. Soon you might find that they congregate around a certain topic, and you could create a story collection, or a memoir of linked essays.

Prompt:

Write down one story a grandparent told you from his or her life.

Finding Focus

F inding focus in your writing is a big challenge, especially when you're writing a personal narrative. How do you whittle down a big life into one small story?

Here are some techniques:

- Use a metaphor as a vehicle.

- Create a mission statement for your piece.

- Give the most space in your piece to the main topic (don't let tangents take over the story).

- Set up the topic in the beginning.

- Make sure the end delivers on the beginning.

Before continuing, please read the story, "The Bed," by Diane Hurles in the Readings section (see page 127). Diane is a former student of mine from StoryStudio Chicago. The rest of this chapter refers to features of this story and won't make much sense if you haven't read it.

Use a Metaphor.

"The Bed" illustrates nicely how you can craft a succinct, stand-alone story that captures so much of a big life story—in her case, the story of losing her mother when she was twelve. Many things pile into that story: What happened before her mother got sick, what happened after the illness took over, her relationship with the grandmother, her father and siblings, the aftermath of her mother's death. From all of that, how do you shape a story without it growing all kinds of tangents?

Diane began writing this story in her fifties, when she was going through boxes after moving to Chicago and found a letter her mother had written for a mother-daughter banquet. This letter brought up a slew of memories, and Diane marveled at how her mother had managed to participate even though she was bedridden. By that time, her mother's hospital bed was installed in the family dining room and had become the center for family life. So, while Diane began writing the piece about the letter, it morphed into a piece about the bed.

The bed became the metaphor not only for her mother's illness but also for her mother's skill at managing some semblance of motherhood from the bed. Focusing on the bed and seeing the story from that perspective shaped this story: As Diane edited, she took out anything that did not relate to the bed, saving it for another essay.

Parking Lots: You can write about one topic, and, as you are writing, stuff comes up that you never consciously carried around. Be sure to jot down all these things and put them in a Parking Lot document (see The Parking Lot Tool chapter). They might come in handy later!

Create a mission statement.

Remember English composition class? Coming up with a thesis statement helps you, and ultimately your reader, understand what your piece is about. I'm not saying that you need a formulaic thesis statement at the end of your first paragraph as you would in a classic five-paragraph persuasive essay. Rather, as you set out to write, it is useful to have a mission statement that answers the question:

What do I want to achieve with this piece?

Your mission statement can be simple:

This piece is about_____.

Once you have your mission statement, make a list of scenes that show what you are trying to capture. List episodes from family history or family life that relate to the story you're aiming to tell.

One of my students was writing about her mother being in the hospital. She noticed that her mother's hospitalization was harder on the rest of the family than it was on the mother. Full of energy, other family members were buzzing around, while her mother was content being still. My student was struck by that (we should always write about things that impress us, things we puzzle about) because she felt it showed something essential about her mother in contrast to the rest of the family. She realized that over the years, her mom had perfected the art of being still and observing. She loved sitting quietly in a corner reading, while her husband had to be busy in the yard. That was her preferred state of being. Therefore, being grounded during the hospital stay was easy for the mom and hard for the rest of the family.

As we were working on this piece, my student was trying to come up with different scenes to put in. It helped to have her mission statement ("This piece is about my mom's art of being still.") as a guide to sift through all the family scenes in her memory to pick the ones that fit this story.

I like to envision my mission statement for a story as functioning like a clothesline. What am I going to hang on it that'll fit the story?

A Word on Tangents

With all this emphasis on focusing on the topic, I have to admit that tangents in stories are sometimes the juiciest part. Not everything in your piece needs to relate to your mission statement.

You need to be careful about how much real estate you give a tangent.

Real estate is the space in your story. How many paragraphs or pages you devote to a topic indicates emphasis to your reader. The more space you give an episode, the more likely your reader will take that to be the main topic. If you go off on a tangent, and that tangent gets three pages in a five-page essay, then that tangent has taken over the story. Your topic has clearly become something different from what you started out with. This is fine; you just have to jigger your piece to fit this new topic and put the old one in a parking lot—or have it live on in small tangents.

In fact, it happens often that we start writing about one thing and end up somewhere completely different. As you write, ideas or memories float to the surface that you weren't even aware of, and then you just have to write two stories instead of one.

The more you write, the more ideas you will have.

I have often found that pure brainstorming by myself is not that helpful because I am actively, i.e., consciously, thinking about something. If I brainstorm with someone else, it can be more fruitful, but then I am also interacting, creating a conversation. I find it more helpful to start writing, beginning with one idea I want to explore, one episode I want to write down, and to see where it leads me.

Once you begin, all kinds of magic will happen. That's the creative process.

To maintain focus, be mindful of how you begin and end your story. Your beginning is the reader's signpost: This is what this piece is about.

Set Up Your Topic in the Beginning.

Diane's story "The Bed" gives us the topic right away:

> "My mother's illness defined my childhood from the time I was seven years old."

This beginning sets the mood of the piece as it succinctly indicates the topic—illness. We know this is not going to be a jolly story, even if it might have comic moments. It also lets us know that this story is told from the perspective of a child. Notice that the main vehicle of the story, the bed, is not introduced this early. Rather, it is developed and becomes part of the movement in the story.

As you write and figure out what you are writing about, make sure you set up the topic in the beginning. This might require several rewrites. Quite often, we need to write ourselves into the story, so a draft might begin with something entirely different from what the topic turns out to be in the final version.

Side note: Beware of beginning with a weather report: "It was a sunny day, and I was walking down the street." This is fine for your first draft. When you revise, take out the weather report unless the weather is important in your story. One of my students was writing a story set in the blizzard that shut down Chicago in February 2011. In that case, beginning with the snowstorm was appropriate, as it was a main character in the story.

The End Has to Deliver.

Your ending has to deliver on what you promised in the beginning, keeping a tight focus on the topic.

In the example of "The Bed," the topic and the mood are picked up again at the end, bringing the story full circle. This provides a satisfying wrap-up for the reader:

> "We couldn't see beyond the bed."

At the end, the bed takes center stage, as that is the role it slowly assumed in the story.

One easy way to deliver on the beginning is to loop back, not by restating the beginning, but by picking up the theme and ideally projecting toward the future (the story beyond the story). Most of the time this works, even if it's formulaic.

In "The Bed," Diane did not mention the bed in the first paragraph, but throughout the piece the bed became the metaphor for the illness, and for how this family dealt with it. At the end, the bed isn't even there anymore, yet it still dominates the room and the bereaved family's life. Nevertheless, in that little sentence, "We couldn't see beyond the bed," a "yet" is implied. We feel that life goes on, and eventually the family *will* see beyond the bed.

Prompt:

Can you think of an object, an item, that was symbolic for how your family dealt with a challenge, a calamity? Write about that.

The Parking Lot Tool

Quite often, we need to shorten a piece to meet a word count or simply to focus it. However, we tend to be scared to delete words we have already put down, passages we labored over that we now find are too much of a tangent or off topic.

The popular writing advice, "Kill your darlings," i.e., eliminating phrases you worked hard on that nevertheless don't lend anything to the story, is understandably hard to execute.

This is where the parking lot tool comes in.

It works like this: When I am trimming a piece of writing, I open another document, give it the same file name as the piece I am editing, and add the words "parking lot." Then, when I cut passages, I paste them into the parking lot document rather than deleting them. That way, the trimming goes much faster because I can be harsher.

Those precious passages are not lost; they are just "parked."

Occasionally, I have gone back and put something in again that I had previously taken out. After all, the editorial process is fickle. As you trim, you home in on a piece's meaning, and sometimes a passage you thought should be cut actually needs to be in there. Thanks to the parking lot document, it is not lost.

I never delete my parking lot files.

Once in a while, when I work on another piece, I get that keen sense of having already written this. Sure enough, I find it in a parking lot (the document search function is a beautiful thing!). Most of the time, however, a parking lot document never gets looked at again once its corresponding piece is finished.

Sometimes, while I am editing, the parking lot document gets fuller and fuller, meaning I have cut a lot, but I still haven't reached the required word count. With a recent essay I was working on, I started with about 1,300 words that I trimmed to 878, which was still short of the required range of 700–800 words. At that point, I sent the piece to my daughter. She can see what I cannot. Sometimes she'll ask me, despite all the cutting, to elaborate on something I took out. Thankfully, all the cuts are still in the parking lot, ready to be evaluated again.

Sources

(pencil illustration)

F amily history comes to us from three main sources: oral history, documents, and research.

Oral history

Oral history is composed of the stories relatives have told you but no one took the time to write down. When you actually write down one of those stories, you will often find that there are holes, things you don't remember. If the purveyor of the story is still alive, go ask them to retell it to you and let them know you want to capture it. Ask follow-up questions right then and there. If the storyteller doesn't remember, leave a blank that you can fill in later. The important thing is to keep going and get this one story down on paper. You could also record him or her, which will be a priceless family record in and of itself. You can easily do this with any smartphone, which will allow you to transcribe the interview later and listen to it again and again if necessary. If the person who used to tell that story isn't alive anymore, or doesn't want to talk about it, write down what you know. Then try to fill the holes through your own research by asking other relatives for their version of the story or employing more traditional research approaches, as outlined in this chapter.

Documents

Documents are basically any piece of paper (actual or virtual) from your family's past, including letters, diaries, journals, memoirs a family member wrote, or even other books they wrote. A book always tells you something about the author, even if it's not autobiographical. For example, I was thrilled when I found a book of my great-grandfather's children's stories on eBay, simply by typing in his name. Holding the small, blue, cloth-bound volume of Peter Rabbit-like stories in my hand gave me a direct connection to my great-grandfather. It was also illuminating to learn that this teacher, who always looked rather stern in family portraits, wrote amusing, moral-filled stories for children in his spare time.

Photos can be another great source. As the cliché goes, a picture is worth a thousand words. A photo can be a great foundation for a story; one example is Larry Palmer's "Urshel–the Beautiful Lost Sheep" that was inspired by a family portrait.

Research

Research leads many people to get interested in their family history. If that's the case for you, and you already have a ton of research, your task is to find the compelling stories. On the other hand, if you're beginning with a particular story you want to tell, research will help you fill the holes of family history, ideally anyway, because you can't always find what you are looking for. Research can entail a lot of different things, from booking an appointment at a historical archive, to looking into eyewitness accounts of a deportation, to requesting a sister's medical records from a hospital, to visiting the town your great-grandparents moved to in the Canadian Prairie. The chapters on The Importance of Research and Filling in the Blanks of My Jewish Family History dive into the topic of research.

Prompt:

Randomly pull a photograph from one of your boxes, piles, or drawers of family photographs and describe the setting, the time this was taken, the people in the photo and your relationship to them. If you have no idea who the people in the photo are, hone your description skills by writing about the image, then speculate what's going on in it, or make a list of questions.

Interviews

Most of the time, we think of family history in terms of the dead, but if you should be so lucky that your grandparents or other elders are still alive, take the time to try to capture some of their memories. Now, that sounds easier than it might be. Not everyone is a storyteller who conceives of his or her life that way. Furthermore, it can be awkward to hit people up for their stories.

You have to find the right entry point to interview someone, and you have to be well prepared.

When I was trying to round out some of my great-aunt's story, I happened to be visiting her daughter, by then an old lady in a nursing home. I was close to her, but I still couldn't, out of the blue, ask her what life had been like as a half-Jewish adolescent under the Nazis. However, while we were talking about her flimsy bed linens, she brought up her father's textile business, and that gave me an opening. I knew, from other family stories, that her Gentile mother had been able to save her father's "Jewish" business after the Nazi takeover of Czechoslovakia. Therefore, I was prepared to ask questions about the business, which easily led to a wider conversation about life under the Nazis.

Before you interview someone, study the family tree, dig out old photos, reread letters, memoirs, etc.

Interviewing is its own art, and I am by no means an expert, but here are some approaches I have seen work, specifically in getting relatives to share their stories:

- **Keep asking**.

  I once sat at a conference next to a white-haired lady, when we were tasked to interview each other. I began asking her the usual biographical questions. Her answers were pretty run-of-the-mill, born here, gone to school there, lived here, lived there, married so-and-so, until I asked how many kids she had. She replied, "Well, I had four but the two oldest died as babies." Four kids and two died as babies? There was the story! Now there was a whole lot I wanted to know from her—not only what happened, but how did she deal with that double tragedy? I was a young mother myself at the time, so that was most interesting to me; that was where I could learn from her. Tragedy makes for a sad, but not necessarily interesting, story. Merely relating what happened results in an anecdote, hopefully an engaging one, but that's it. There's no more substance. How someone dealt with tragedy is interesting because that's where the reader can learn something. How someone dealt with tragedy is also what affects the next generation—in the case of this individual, what kind of mother did she become to the children who did survive?

• **Ask about a passion.**

In the example above, I asked standard biographical questions, and those are important to at least get the milestones right, but if you don't hit a stunning story like I did, and you're not talking to someone who's a natural storyteller, ask them about something they love and care about deeply. It might be grandma's love for crocheting—her afghans are in every relative's living room. (This is the connection to the present and why the story of the afghans might be interesting.) So ask: How did she learn to crochet? Why does she make afghans, not doilies? Keep asking, using different angles. Sooner or later, you'll hit on something interesting. At the very least, you'll be able to tell the story of the afghans. Here's another example: Rebecca McClanahan, one of my MFA workshop leaders, was trying to get more family history out of her dad, but he was the taciturn type. Then she had the brilliant idea to ask him about all the cars he ever owned, and, all of a sudden, he had a lot to say. She ended up with the story of his life told through the lens of his cars. Her poem "My Father's Cadillac" is the result.

- **Ask "thick" questions**. A thick question requires at least a full sentence in reply, often more. Some examples:

    - What was your favorite book as a child?

    - What is your favorite book?

    - What is your favorite fairy tale?

    - Who was your favorite relative and why?

    - How did you pick your wedding dress?

    - Why do you like living in your city/town/ village?

    - What dish did your mom fix that you hated?

- **Dig for the meaning**. Remember that the story itself, namely the who, what, when, and where, is just the skeleton. You are looking for the meaning because therein lies the meat that makes this story interesting to you and hopefully others in your family. So keep on digging as you pursue a story. Ask questions like:

  - Why did you do that?

  - How did that make you feel?

Other methods to get stories out of relatives:

- **Look through a photo album** with them and ask who is who (label photos if they don't have decent captions), and take notes on their reminiscences.

- **Sift through a box of old photographs** and ask them to help label and date photos.

- **Go on a tour of their childhood neighborhood** with them, making note of addresses, taking pictures of buildings, and jotting down whatever stories emerge. This might become a nice local history piece. In the aftermath of Hurricane Harvey, for example, Sandi Wisenberg wrote about the demise of the Houston neighborhood where she grew up: "After Harvey, A Requiem for Jewish Houston." Take a video of the excursion that you can share with the rest of the family. You could also use the footage as evidence in your research.

- **Travel to a place of significance in their lives** with them. A year before my mother-in-law passed away, my husband and I traveled to France with her, our three kids, and her wheelchair in tow and visited the village where she had been hidden as a child during the Holocaust. She hadn't been there since 1946. It was priceless to witness her recall where the outhouse had been, how she and her sister had been scared of the rats, how her brothers told them ghost stories about the little cemetery there. That visit gave me the material for the chapter "Briosne" in my book.

Prompt:

Pick one family story you are curious about and interview a relative.

Using Other Voices

A s with tangents, be careful when you use someone else's voice. By this, I don't mean dialogue but
rather quoting a diary entry or citing a letter. In
family stories in particular, it adds texture and authenticity
to quote a letter or someone you interviewed. Just be aware
that if you do, you are handing the microphone to someone
else. Don't hand it over for too long because then it becomes
that person's story.

The narrator holds together any personal narrative.

Therefore, you don't want someone else to become the narrator unless you want to tell the story from their perspective.
That is fine, too, but then you have to be conscious of that
decision.

Two well-done examples of using old letters or diary entries to round out historical context in a memoir are the
following:

- Russell Baker's Pulitzer Prize-winning memoir
  Growing Up showcased his particularly skillful use

of Depression-era letters from his mother's suitor Olaf.

- Rebecca McClanahan's *The Tribal Knot* used not only family letters going back to the Civil War era but also her great-aunt's diary entries to portray life in a primitive cabin in rural Indiana.

I know from my own experience that it can be hard to find the right way to use materials like letters or diaries, or even someone else's memoirs. It might take several go-arounds until you figure out an approach that works well. In my initial drafts of *Jumping Over Shadows*, I simply quoted the most telling passages from my grandfather's memoirs. Many of the people reading those first iterations balked at that. Who is this guy? Why is he suddenly talking to us? The story didn't flow until I learned to transform his writings into a third-person narrative. This allowed me to provide more context where needed, yet continue to narrate from his perspective. Telling the story of the past in third person from my grandfather's point-of-view clearly distinguished that thread from my own, first-person, more present-day one. In general, it is hard to pull off two first-person narrators in one piece of writing, as the two "I's" are challenging for the reader to separate.

Prompt:

Pick one story from a relative's past, such as something your father or mother told you, and write it in third person.

Transforming Oral History into a Scene

✏

U sing an example from my memoir *Jumping Over Shadows*, I want to show you how I transformed a story my Aunt Herta had told me into a scene in the book. Please read the "Queen of the Night" excerpt in the Readings section (see page 135) before moving on.

The first paragraph in "Queen of the Night" is simply exposition, offering a short summary of the role my grandfather, "der Onkel," played in the lives of his niece and nephew, Herta and Ludwig. It also orients the reader in time—from the first sentence, we know this episode is happening before 1932.

The second paragraph moves into the particular story. The first sentence is still general but tells us something about the main character: "He also grew cacti." It grounds us in place by giving us a glimpse of the inside of his apartment: "in the white light of the turret room overlooking Tuchplatz." This description, strictly speaking, is conjecture, as I have not been inside that apartment. But I have been to the building. I know that turret faces southeast, is unobstructed by other buildings, and gets plenty of light. Incidentally, the current occupants still grow plants on the windowsill in that turret.

Then we move into the action, into the scene:

- "One summer night" - specific time

- "After Herta and Ludwig had already been tucked into bed" - tells us who the main characters are

- "tucked" - hint that we are in a family environment and are dealing with younger children

- "Their doorbell rang" - action! Something happens

- "Shortly thereafter, Resi came into their room and said, 'Come on, you two, get dressed again. The Uncle wants us to come over. He has something special to show us.'" - Here, another character enters, and the unusual situation is established ("get dressed again"). The reader's anticipation is heightened: "He has something special to show us." Now we are curious, along with the kids, as to what that could be.

From then on, the scene develops. People are on the move and talking to one another. Note how sensory details like "Herta's clogs booming through the stairwell" help create a three-dimensional space that the reader can feel, see, hear, and, thus, enter. I took the liberty here to have Herta wear clogs on that particular night. That wasn't part of the story she used to tell, but I knew from other stories that she had clogs. I have been in that stairway, so I know that it has stone steps on which wooden shoes would make a lot of noise. I used my knowledge of her life and of the place to round out this scene.

The interaction between the people in this story is based on Herta's telling of it, but also on what I know about the characters. Resi was the kind of person who would flatter her brother about the wonderful scent of the Queen of the Night, whereas Guido would be more truthful. Herta and Ludwig, being kids, cared more about the unusual nightly outing and whether it was true that the cactus bloomed for only one night (hence, Herta insisting on checking the next day). I knew my grandfather was fastidious and took his photography seriously. He would be exacting when taking photos of that rare cactus blossom.

When I wrote the first draft of this scene, I realized I had no idea what that Queen of the Night cactus actually looked like and whether indeed it blossoms the way Herta had told me. That's where research comes in (see The Importance of Research). Thankfully, in this day and age, I only had to google "Queen of the Night cactus," and I immediately found images that helped me describe it.

Whatever you can google, your reader can, too.

Therefore, we have to double-check everything that can be found on the internet.

Double-checking family stories like these also helps you determine how reliable your family storytellers are. The Queen of the Night story could easily have been exaggerated, but it wasn't. That told me that Herta was a fairly reliable storyteller.

The chapter ends with the demise of the blossom but also a short musing:

"This nocturnal excursion must have happened in 1930 or 1931, when Herta was old enough to remember; when . . ." — this is a projection forward, a short interpretation of this time in the larger context of their lives, which I, with the hindsight I have, can provide.

Lastly, why tell this particular story? Why take the trouble to create it as a scene? While I do urge you to write in scene as much as possible, you have to be judicious about it:

"Remember the wisdom of the child: Make a scene when you really want everyone's full attention."
—Jerome Stern, *Making Shapely Fiction*

You only write in scene when it is something important. Background information should not be conveyed as a scene but in exposition because it does not have the same level of importance within the story as the forward-moving action.

Having read my "Queen of the Night" scene, what did you learn about the characters, and where do you think this story is headed next?

Analyzing my own writing is a bit awkward, but I would say I wrote the "Queen of the Night" story as a scene because:

- It shows the fairly easygoing interaction within this family before the hard times came around.

- It shows that they are the kind of family who gets along with one another and cares about the finer things of life.

- In this episode, they could still concern themselves with frivolities and weren't focused on survival.

- The short life of the blossom evokes their own brief carefree life.

- Its quick death is symbolic of the impending doom.

Prompt:

Write down one story someone in your family told you. Then try to turn it into a scene as if you were staging a play. Who are the actors? What are they wearing? What day and time is it? Where in the world are they? What do the surroundings look like? What are they saying to one another? Use your knowledge of the characters to round out the scene, research the rest, and see what you can piece together.

The Importance of Research

✏️

Research leads many people to want to write their family history. But to create compelling stories, keep in mind that:

Just because you discovered something doesn't mean it needs to be a story.

An entire research trip might end up being one sentence in your story. That's OK because the research gives you the authority to know what you are talking about. Writing the story, you need to select carefully which facts need to be in there to move it forward.

There are many types of research to consider:
- Paper: libraries, archives, private papers, medical records
- Living people: see chapter on Interviews
- Electronic: internet, social media, GPS
- Visual: photos, X-rays, blueprints
- Audio: music, specific sounds, recorded voices
- Institutions: historical museums, collections, archives
- Experiential: location, recreating an experience

Research Trips

Before going on a research trip, prepare for it as much as you can. I am guilty myself of not always preparing thoroughly, much to my regret. On my most recent trip to my grandparents' hometown of Liberec (Reichenberg) in the Czech Republic, a prominent location in *Jumping Over Shadows*, my sister and I decided to drive to the old mill our great-great-grandparents used to own. Last we knew, from my visit there fourteen years prior, it had been a ruin.

Before embarking on that trip, I should have reread our grandmother's handwritten memoirs to see if she mentioned the mill. Turns out she did. Unfortunately, I only found that information later when I dug out what she had written to brush up on the history as I was writing a blog post about our visit: "Why Returning to Our Roots Is So Meaningful."

My grandmother's memoirs are only fifteen pages, but they held valuable clues as to who owned what, how they had traveled to the mill when no one had a car, and all that went on there. She also wrote about a hill opposite the mill that had 100 steps leading to a little chapel at the top. She wrote about how she loved to run up there as a kid—it was the first thing she would do upon arriving for her summer vacation! My internet image and Google Maps search showed me that those steps were still there.

I could have kicked myself! My sister and I could have run up those steps, just as our grandmother had done as a kid! Who knows what we would have seen from up there? At the very least, we could have had the same experience. I could have taken photos to complement my grandmother's memories. But I missed that opportunity because I didn't do my homework! (I am not going to be back in the Czech Republic any time soon.)

On a prior research trip for the book, I had a list of the locations I wanted to visit. Once on site, it's easy to get distracted by other attractions or to get bogged down by the challenges of travel.

While on a research trip, it is also a good idea to plan a day to just write if you can. Had I tried to write that blog post right after the visit to the mill, I would have found the passage about those steps, and we could have gone back to look for them.

Research goes in circles. As you write, you discover more things you need to know.

Research entails double-checking everything: birth dates, marriage dates, death certificates, historic events, land deeds, maps for street names, etc.

Anything someone else can verify, you need to verify.

If you are writing about a specific place, for example, other people will know their way around there too. If you get something wrong, you immediately lose your credibility as a writer.

An experience early on in my writing of *Jumping Over Shadows* drove that idea home with me. I was attending an alumni conference of my MFA program, and I had submitted a chapter about my grandparents' lives in Liberec to a manuscript workshop. As my fellow workshop participants were discussing my manuscript, one woman said that my writing about Liberec had been particularly meaningful to her because she had lived there when her husband, a Czech architect, taught in Liberec. Wow! How likely was it that in a workshop in Charlotte, NC, someone who knew Liberec intimately would be in the same workshop with me? Thankfully, she found no fault with my depictions, and I breathed a sigh of relief. Later, we reminisced about some of the locations. I was relieved that my visits to Liberec had paid off and that I had learned enough about the town to describe it in such a way that someone who lived there would be satisfied.

Prompt:

Take a research trip. Prepare a list of what you want to find out. It could be as easy as visiting your local public library to find pertinent history books or stopping at a cemetery to take pictures of a grave. It could be as elaborate as visiting a grandparent's childhood neighborhood or town. It could be a visit to an archive to find more historical material. The main thing is to get out there and do a little digging!

Filling in the Blanks of My Jewish Family History

✎

Many a reader or interviewer has told me they were amazed at the amount of research that went into my book. "Wasn't that hard?" they would ask. Truth be told, I loved the research, even if research can be quite frustrating. You don't always find what you expect. Often, you simply have to deal with the void. Without research, I could not have told my great-aunt's story, and I could not have written *Jumping Over Shadows* the way I did.

I always knew that my German great-aunt Resi had been married to a Jewish man, Guido Knina, in Czechoslovakia before World War II. However, it wasn't until I, living in post-WWII Germany, fell in love with a Jewish man that I wanted to know more about Resi's story. When I decided that this love between a German woman and a Jewish man happening twice in my family would make a good book, I had to fill in the blanks.

What had really happened to my Jewish great-uncle? What had happened to this couple when the Nuremberg Laws, prohibiting marriages between "Aryans" and "non-Aryans," had taken effect in 1938?

Growing up, I was close to the daughter of this marriage, my dad's first cousin Herta. She told me many family stories, such as the one about the Queen of the Night cactus—as did my grandmother, who was a gifted storyteller. Nevertheless, being aware of family stories is one thing; being able to retell them within their historical context is another.

Fit family lore into a historical timeframe.

When I traveled to Liberec for the first time in 2002 and told Herta about a beautiful café there, she said, "Oh yes, the Café Post! My father loved to go there on Sunday mornings. My mother didn't like this, but that was his habit. Until he couldn't go anymore. That's how things were then."

"That's how things were then." By this, she meant that her father, Guido Knina, couldn't go to the Café Post anymore because he was a Jew. Once that area of Czechoslovakia was annexed by Hitler after the Munich Agreement in 1938, the laws of the German Reich applied. Jews were banned from public places like cafés. But Herta didn't tell me that. I had to supply that historical context myself.

On another occasion she mentioned, "I always wanted to go to university; I would have loved that. In those days, it wasn't possible, so what could I do?" Characteristically, she did not explain that in the 1940s, in a Czechoslovakia annexed by Nazi Germany, she was not able to study because, classified as a half-Jew, she was barred from institutions of higher education. Only when I read my grandfather's memoirs did I find out he had arranged for her to attend the Handelsakademie (Academy of Commerce), even though technically she was barred from that too. But the principal was a cousin of my grandmother, and he agreed to let Herta attend unregistered.

Research the wider community.

I based the reconstruction of my great-aunt's story on my grandfather's memoirs, and specifically his chapter about his sister. However, he only recorded the intersections of Jewish and gentile life as they affected him. I needed to fill in the blanks if I wanted to contrast my story with my great-aunt's. Who had her husband been? Who had his family been before they were connected with my family?

My first find, on the German eBay site, was the book *Reichenberg*, published in Augsburg in 1974. It included a chapter on "The Israelite Cultural Community in Reichenberg." Their history was the usual sordid tale of rights granted to Jews and then rescinded, coupled with various harassments, until in 1860 Jews were given full citizenship by Austro-Hungarian Emperor Franz Josef. Then 30 Jewish families took up permanent residence in Reichenberg, a well-to-do hub for textile and glass manufacturing and trade.

While this chapter didn't give me specifics on any Jewish families, it did feature an image of the "temple of the Israelite community." It also cited the image's source, and that presented another thread for me to follow. Promptly I found an article by Dr. Emil Hofmann, "Geschichte der Juden in Reichenberg," published in 1934, on Jewishgen.org.

Here I struck gold: "J.L. Knina" was listed as a member of the temple's building committee. "J.L. Knina" stood for Joachim Ludwig Knina, father of my great-uncle Guido Knina, which I knew from the family tree in my grandfather's memoirs. Further on, in a chapter titled "Jews in Non-Jewish Organizations," I found Guido himself:

"In 1919, Guido Knina was elected to the town council for the Social Democratic Party and remained there for four years."

From my grandfather's memoirs, I knew that he and Guido had served as city councilmen at the same time. I did not know, however, that Guido had been the first Jew elected to the city council. This was the kind of information that would be noteworthy to a Jewish audience but not to my grandfather. Research was needed to fill in the blanks and find the information that was neither part of family lore nor contained in family documents. Ordering books, viewing them online, or borrowing volumes on Czech history from the library was, however, not enough.

Hit the archives.

On my trip to Reichenberg in 2009, I went to the public library there and asked whether they had newspapers from 1938. I wanted to read reports from that time, so I would be able to recreate what life had been like then. The archivist told me it was unlikely they had any papers because they had a fire at some point, but she did put in a request and told me to return in two hours. When I did, she gesticulated that they did have something. I had to give her my passport as a "security deposit," even though I would only be able to view whatever she had in a reading room. Then she handed me a ledger of yellowed newspapers from 1938. Thankfully, I could read the old Gothic-style German print.

Reading these newspapers, I came face-to-face with life as it had been back then, unfiltered by hindsight. Even though from September 1938 on, *Die Zeit*, Reichenberg's city newspaper, had been a Nazi organ, it was still a fascinating read. The November 11, 1938 edition gleefully described the destruction of Reichenberg's synagogue during Kristallnacht. An image of the burned-out synagogue featured the caption: "Only the walls are left standing—the population protests the Jewish murderous attack." This referred to the pretext for the Kristallnacht pogrom, namely the assassination of German diplomat Ernst vom Rath by Herschel Grynszpan, a seventeen-year-old Polish Jew, in Paris on November 7, 1938.

As far as I know, my great-uncle Guido never found out that the synagogue his father helped build went up in flames. He was already in a sanatorium, suffering from diabetes, in and out of consciousness. My grandmother spent that day at his bedside. By that time, he and my great-aunt Resi were divorced, presumably so she, the "Aryan," could continue to run his textile business, save the family's livelihood, and ferry her half-Jewish children through the Nazi inferno.

In 2012, when my manuscript was already finished, another book on the history of the Jews of Reichenberg was published: *Reichenberg und seine jüdischen Bürger* by Isa Engelmann. Thankfully for my project, it confirmed the family story that Guido's wife, my great-aunt Theresia (called "Resi" by the family), took over the business Joachim Ludwig Knina had founded in 1878 and that Guido (his son) had run until 1938:

> "We should also mention here the company J.L. Knina, probably Reichenberg's oldest wholesaler for manufactured goods, founded in 1878 by the Prague Merchant Joachim Ludwig Knina (1845-1903), which from 1938 on was run by his daughter-in-law Theresia Knina, who wasn't subject to the racial laws."

To keep up appearances, Resi had no contact with Guido after the divorce. Instead, my grandparents cared for him. They bribed the staff so he could stay in the sanatorium, as Jews were barred from all kinds of institutions by then. When he passed away in December 1938, they arranged for his funeral.

It is, of course, nice when history books confirm what your family has been telling you, but you owe it to your project to double-check. If you find family stories contradicted, you need to investigate. Then the quest to figure out the real story can become the story you tell, or the story of why your family told a different story becomes the story. There's always a story to tell—it just might not be the one you thought you were telling.

No document, no artifact, tells the whole story.

Graves are their own form of documentation. Many years after Guido's death, his son Ludwig, the only relative to remain in Reichenberg, had my family's and Guido's graves put together because, after the war, German gravestones were often vandalized in Czechoslovakia. Nowadays, the family gravestone only reads "Rodina Kninova" (Family Knia). Unless you request to see the register for this grave, which I did, you wouldn't know that my relatives with the last name Berndt are also buried there.

Again, one piece of evidence, namely the grave, told only part of the story. The associated register tells another. Even together, they are not the whole story. Nowhere, except in my family's oral history, will you find that Guido, buried there, was Jewish.

It all needs to come together—artifacts, documents, and lore—to round out the picture.

Even then, I am not convinced that it is the whole story. What remains of a life, of all lives, is always fragments. Once a subsequent generation finds these fragments, it depends on how they piece them together, as to what story might be told of the past.

Prompt:

Make a list of all the graves of your family that you know about. In which cemeteries are they buried and why? Provide directions to graves and include pictures if you have any. Is there one grave you can write a story about?

What if People Are Already Dead?

You can do all the things I mentioned in the previous chapter in order to round out or even find stories, but it will, of course, be harder when your relatives aren't around anymore to guide you and supply details of the story.

Photographs can inform stories, so can locations. I could have never written my great-aunt's story without visiting my grandparents' and her hometown in the Czech Republic. Visits themselves can become a story, i.e., you can tell the story of your discoveries, your quest. Many a family memoir is written like that. *The Hare with Amber Eyes* by Edmund De Waal is one of the most brilliant examples. De Waal uses his quest to guide the reader through a multi-generational story and make it relevant to our times.

If you can't ask anyone else about the past, mine your own memories.

Free writing is a good technique to delve into your own memory.

It simply means choosing a topic that you're struggling with, setting a timer, and writing down whatever comes to mind.

Ideally, write by hand. Handwriting is a more organic process that engages your brain more fully. Don't edit; don't second guess. Just write.

Fiction writers use this technique, for example, to figure out what a character might want. It is crucial that you write without overthinking; just jot down whatever comes to mind. This sounds easier than it is. Be sure to keep your hand moving.

Many a time, things only occur to us while we are engaged in writing. Free writing is a technique; thus, it only works when you actually do it—not when you think about it. You need to write.

Prompt:

Set a timer for ten minutes and free write about a topic or a person from your family history you would like to know more about.

When Legend and Research Collide

W̲hat are you supposed to do when your research debunks a family legend? Or when lore is proven wrong by historical fact?

What if you find that a great-great-uncle who was lauded in his obituary to have fought under Napoleon in the Moscow campaign is instead listed in regiment rosters as having fought in a later, less interesting campaign? What if the POW story that was always told about him cannot be true, given these new facts?

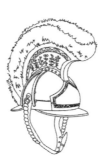

First of all, tread lightly: Historical fact isn't necessarily historical fact. A document can be false.

As I stated before, a document tells one story but never the whole story.

Take the example of the ledger of my family's grave in Liberec: As I pointed out, while the ledger does list all the people that are, to the best of my knowledge, buried there, it gives no evidence that one of them, my great-uncle Guido, was Jewish. And why should it?

Furthermore, documents can be falsified for various reasons. People changed names, listed wrong information, made deliberate omissions. How many stories have we heard of WWII veterans who pretended to be older just so they could join the military?

If you're grappling with a historical discovery that seems to contradict the family story and documents, try to find corroborating evidence to verify what you have found. Quite often, we run into dead ends with challenges like these, as historical records are limited. If you've done as much as you can there, I would say:

Make your quandary the story.

Write a piece in which you relate the new historical facts you found, why you believe they are correct, how they contrast with family lore, and what you are left with. What is obviously not true, or what might be true but cannot be verified?

It would also be worth reflecting on why the family created the legend, if indeed they did.

Why would your ancestors have constructed a pack of lies? What were they trying to conceal? Achieve? That could be the really interesting part.

Prompt:

Is there an event in your family history for which people tell different versions? Write down those different versions and try to tie them together with your own interpretation, then perhaps do some research to see which version you can verify.

Practical Stuff: How to Approach Your Project

Don't Worry About Perfection

✐

When I taught a memoir workshop at the Hemingway Birthplace Home, the ninety-one-year-old lady who had originally overseen the restoration of the house was one of my students. I was writer-in-residence at the time with a studio in the attic, where I typically spent the day working before teaching the workshop in the evening. She'd call me before class to instruct me which table to bring up from the basement to put our refreshments on. At the end of class, she'd hurry off to climb the steep stairs to the second floor to make sure all the lights were turned off.

I was a bit intimidated to be teaching someone who could be my grandmother. When participants shared why they were taking the class, she said that her daughter had told her not to worry about who of her six children would get the china but to write down some of the stories only she knew. However, when her turn came to submit a draft to the workshop, she didn't bring anything. When I later challenged her why she hadn't, she sheepishly admitted that she just couldn't write anything down.

"You see," she said, "I'm the only one who remembers my grandfather. Whatever I write down is going to be it. It has to be perfect, and I just don't know how to do that."

That made sense, but . . .

I replied, "Yes, but if you don't put anything down, there will be nothing."

Clearly, she wanted help. Even though the class had wrapped up, I felt the urgency that, at ninety-one, she'd better get to it. I suggested we meet for lunch and that she bring some notes. We'd work together on whatever she'd written down.

Sure enough, when we met a few weeks later, she brought a legal pad with a few sheets full of her elegant handwriting. She read them to me. They were beautiful reminiscences of her Wisconsin childhood at her grandparents' farm. Even if she didn't go any further than what she had written on that legal pad, she now had something. Her grandfather was down on paper.

Anything is better than nothing.

Sometimes, handwriting is all that is needed, for it captures not only the story but also the unique personality of the writer. No two handwritings are alike, and thus handwriting is one brilliant way to transmit our individuality for generations to come. A few handwritten notes can be a treasure down the line.

Prompt:

Type up a relative's handwritten memories, a letter, or recipe cards. Handwriting is often hard to read by the following generations, so making it accessible is a worthwhile endeavor. You could even create a booklet with the handwritten version and the transcript side by side, preserving the handwriting's unique character. There are many terrific online sites to help you create books. If you have no handwritten notes from others to transcribe, take the time to handwrite one of your own.

Where to Begin

s with any writing project, the question of where to start can be paralyzing. The sheer volume of material might be overwhelming (loads of photos, piles of documents, a plethora of stories). Or perhaps the opposite is true: What you know for sure is so scant you wonder whether you can make anything of it. What to do?

After serving on a memoir panel at a literary event in Minneapolis, I ended up chatting with an attendee who told me her mother had recently passed away and left her with boxes of journals and letters. It included the journal her grandmother had kept as a young wife in the Minnesota backwoods in the 1930s. She wanted to do something with all this, but where to start? As we spoke, I made several suggestions, all of which she seemed to put on a mental list of ideas. It wasn't until we'd talked for a while that she mentioned she had gotten pregnant at sixteen and she found, in her mother's diary, that her grandparents had fostered a girl who'd also become pregnant at sixteen. That parallel between her life and her grandmother's life was her entry!

Look for stories that repeat themselves within your family.

Clearly, something is going on when a particular pattern appears in more than one generation. The same story repeating itself in my family was the impetus for *Jumping Over Shadows*. Curious about this repetition, I began to write my book, and you can begin to write yours.

Where does the past affect the present?

As mentioned earlier, whatever those who came before us experienced or decided to do has a direct impact on who we are.

Look for events that changed the trajectory of a family.

A grandmother migrated from Southern China to the Philippines; thus, her descendants are now Filipino and Catholic. Why did she move? That would be the story to write, bolstered with historical research where needed.

Begin with an object that encapsulates the then and the now.

Do you still bake fruitcake for Christmas, even though no one in your family likes it, simply because it was your grandmother's recipe, and it means "Christmas" to you? Tell the story of that fruitcake, sensory details and recipe included! Countless people spend years trying to recreate a beloved family recipe, only to fail because the original cook never wrote it down.

Objects are powerful vehicles for storytelling.

Objects that used to belong to a loved one can attain cult status, and they can be great vehicles for storytelling, even when you have little else to go on. I used my father's toiletry bag for years after he passed away. This toiletry bag could serve as a vehicle for telling the stories of all the trips we took together, or his trips as a businessman, or his cologne that always traveled in that bag and still reminds me of him. Objects are powerful vehicles for storytelling.

Prompt:

Write about one object you inherited—ideally, one you still use.

What if Your Material Is Too Rosy?

A t a conference, one of my workshop participants lamented that her mother had only left a happy-go-lucky account of her experiences, while the daughter knew very well it hadn't always been a happy and easy life.

An engaging story thrives on contrast. If a story is only happy, it does not make for a satisfying read, nor does it make a believable story. Therefore, if your source material is too rosy, it is your job to fill in the blanks and provide the contrast.

That's not to say that you cannot write a successful happy memoir, but some shadows have to be woven into a story full of light for it to have texture and depth. Gerald Durrell's *My Family and Other Animals* is a great example of a cheerful family memoir. However, even that story includes squabbles, conflict, discontent, and money troubles.

Also, if someone leaves behind memoirs that only capture an idealized version of her life, ask yourself why she did that. Why did this person feel the need to make her life appear perfect? Answering that question will give you an entry into your subject's inner life. You can build on the contradiction between reality and her account to try and portray her as a character.

Prompt:

Write two pages about a particularly joyful episode in your family's life.

Writing About Others

Writing about real people is probably the number one issue writers of family stories worry about. Frank McCourt, for example, was not able to write his brilliant memoir *Angela's Ashes* until his mother passed away. He knew he would have to write about her affair with her cousin, and he couldn't do that as long as she was alive.

Waiting until relatives are dead is one option. Ellen Douglas did that for *Truth: Four Stories I Am Finally Old Enough to Tell*. Dead people can't sue you, nor can you invade their privacy, and to my knowledge only a famous person's estate might have grounds to come after you for any kind of libel. Furthermore, dead people won't get mad at you or stop talking to you.

What if you don't want to wait until someone is dead? How do you navigate the treacherous waters of writing about others, especially family?

Write first, worry later.

Why? Because **you can never predict how people will react**. For example, when Joe Mackall, author of the memoir *The Last Street Before Cleveland* gave the manuscript to his wife, she got upset at this sentence in the first chapter: "There was the last place I was truly whole." *Had he never felt whole living with her?* He didn't see that one coming (Family First: Panel Discussion, NonfictioNow Conference, Iowa City, November 10, 2005).

Nor did I when I shared a prize-winning essay with my mother. First, she didn't react, and then she called me at work to tell me how upset she was that she wasn't in it. I tried to explain that it was a story about mortality, about my grandmother and my father, both of whom were dead. Since she wasn't dead, there was no point to her being in the story.

"But I am your mother!" she kept saying.

No amount of explanation helped. I realized that as soon as you start explaining your writing to a reader, you've lost the battle. Once it's published, it's out there. Readers can react any which way they want, including your mother.

My mother's huffing about not being in my story brings me to my next point:

Most people love being written about.

It's the same phenomenon as receiving your child's school newsletter: You immediately scan it to see if your child is featured. If not, you lose interest. Similarly, my children usually ask, whenever they hear I've published something, "Am I in it?"

It is human nature to want to be acknowledged, to be seen, to know that we matter, and being written about is a great affirmation of our relevance. Therefore, it is a huge affront to leave someone out of a comprehensive family story. If you have two siblings but only one matters in the book you're writing, you have to at least mention the other sibling's existence, and then move on. This does not apply to short memoirs, such as a story about a brother and sister's favorite place to play, but **in a book-length memoir, all family members need to be mentioned**. Don't "kill" someone by leaving them out.

Reactions are indicative of the relationship.

Often, reactions are indicative of the relationship you have with the person you are writing about. A solid relationship won't fall apart because of your writing; in fact, it might deepen your understanding of each other. On the other hand, a relationship that was already rocky might be blown apart.

Mark Doty's father reportedly didn't speak to him again after Doty sent him the manuscript of his memoir *Firebird*. Sadly, even though their relationship had been precarious, they had just gone through a rapprochement that *Firebird* apparently destroyed (see Doty's article "Return to Sender" in *The Writer's Chronicle*, Oct/Nov 2005).

So ask yourself: What are you willing to risk?

"People's lives are more important than my words," advises Judith Barrington in *Writing the Memoir* (p. 132).

In the same book, Teresa Jordan, author of *Riding the White Horse Home: A Western Family Album*, is quoted as warning: "Writers are users. We use the stories around us. I feel that carries a huge responsibility" (p. 134).

How then does a writer honor this responsibility?

Fictionalizing a true story is not necessarily a way to avoid this responsibility to be mindful of other people's lives.

In an interview with *The Writer's Chronicle* (Summer 2005), Susan Cheever, daughter of John Cheever, relates the following:

> "My father wrote the story called 'The Hartleys'
> in which a little girl, who's obviously me, goes

on a family ski trip—which is, in every detail, the ski trip we took. The little girl gets killed in the ski tow. That, for me, was far more traumatic than if he'd written a nonfiction piece about that ski trip in which he talked about his fears for the little girl. To me, the fiction is much more dangerous, much more painful for the people who it may be based on, than nonfiction. In nonfiction, at least the writer has some obligation to tell what really happened. [...] So, in my family, being fictionalized has been ten million times more painful. That's why, when a student says to me, 'If I did this as fiction it wouldn't hurt the people so much,' I say to them, 'You are wrong. It will hurt them more. Because you as a fiction writer have more power.'"

Incidentally, fictionalizing does not protect you from a possible libel suit. While a successful libel suit against a writer is rare, it is possible if there is enough information about the fictional character that the real person can be identified.

If you feel you're treading on thin ice as you approach a family story, ask yourself, "Which decision is more life enhancing?" Be selective.

Telling all or not telling anything are not the only options.

Often the way you shape a story allows you to leave out complicated stuff. For example, by focusing on small moments between her dying son and herself, my student Susan Wigoda has been able to write her memoir as a series of essays that didn't get bogged down by the larger family story but still beautifully captured the essence of their relationship (see Wigoda, Susan. "Wednesdays and Sundays").

When writing about others, the main challenge is to see and portray real people as multifaceted characters.

This can be especially hard if you are writing about a family member who has a defined role in your life. That person is your father, your mother, your brother. For your story to be engaging, you need to ask yourself:

- Who is (or was) she apart from that?

- What challenges was he facing?

- What motivated her?

The process of seeing a family member as a character in a story can be one of the most rewarding and illuminating by-products of writing memoir.

It leads you to appreciate, for example, who your mother was as a young woman, before she became your mother. If, in writing about her, you manage to step out of your role as her child, you might just develop a compassion towards her that you did not have before.

Nevertheless, it is important to keep in mind that we all have our own perspective. We can only tell our version of the truth. As Michael Steinberg, author of *Still Pitching*, once explained to his mother, "I'm writing about my grandfather, not your father" (see also Steinberg, Michael. "My Life According to Me," *Detroit Metro Times*, December 22, 2004).

Don't share your work until you're 100 percent behind it.

As you write about others, don't show your work to those involved until you have arrived at a final version you're comfortable with. If you showed your father a draft and later deleted a passage he really liked, he'd be disappointed. Likewise, it's not worth possibly upsetting someone with details and stories you're not sure you're going to put out there. Share your work only when you as the writer have arrived at your version of the story, when you are 100 percent comfortable with it. If there's any passage you are queasy about, take it out. Anything iffy will come back to bite you.

When you do show your work to those you are writing about, offer to make changes, but reserve the right to tell your story.

Writing, especially writing stories based on family history, is also a collaborative effort.

Family members can be great fact checkers. At the very least, they need to know that they are being written about. Ideally, they should be comfortable with your portrayal of them. You can, of course, change names to shield their identity, but chances are they will recognize themselves. Always take the high road and involve everyone who is a main character in signing off on the manuscript.

In the end, however, it is your story, and you can't satisfy everyone. You can make sure, however, to be satisfied yourself and to stand 100 percent behind your own work.

Prompt:

Write 1,500 words about your mother. If you have a hard time getting started, make a list of ten things you have from your mother (habits you took on, items you use, traits you inherited) or ten things you can thank your mother for. See where that takes you.

Dealing with Names

How to handle names within the text can be a challenge for memoir writers, and writers of family memoir in particular. First of all, you need to make sure your reader can easily follow the narrative. It should always be clear who the characters are. Providing a family tree can be helpful, but having to refer to it often in order to follow the story can get cumbersome.

Since you're writing about real people, you have to deal with the additional issue of whether or not to use their real names. With this, there are no hard-and-fast rules.

I have found it is best to use proper names for main characters and to refrain from doing so with minor characters.

The goal is to avoid overloading the reader. Not using names is easiest with relatives to whom you can simply refer to by their relationship to you, the narrator, such as "my sister." This works well if the sister doesn't appear often, as the reader immediately knows who she is in relation to the narrator. Since the narrator is the navigator of the story, this makes for good readability. It also protects that relative's privacy. However, if the sister appears more often, referring to her as "my sister" can become annoying; using her name would then be appropriate. If she prefers that you don't use her real name, use a fake one. She will still know who she is, but strangers won't be able to google her based on your story.

For other minor characters who are not relations, it is usually best to refer to them by the role they play in the story. For example, refer to your "first-grade teacher" if that person only appears a few times. However, this becomes awkward and gives the impression you're hiding something if a character appears more often. In that case, it is better to give that character a proper name and introduce him as "Mr. McGrath, my first-grade teacher."

The same should be done to reorient the reader if someone only appears sparingly throughout the text. So you could say "our housekeeper, Mrs. Burns," when she shows up again, instead of expecting the reader to remember who Mrs. Burns was when she appeared ten chapters earlier. Beta readers can be very helpful with this. As the writer, it is hard to tell which characters readers will remember and when they might get confused, so ask your beta readers to indicate where they would appreciate being reminded of who someone is.

Prompt:

Write about how you got your name, whom you are named after (if you are), and why.

My Experience of Writing about Family

A s the author of a family memoir, I am often asked how my family reacted to being written about.

First of all, since *Jumping Over Shadows* is, to a large degree, my own love story, I didn't even shop around the manuscript until my husband had read and approved it. I made whatever changes he wanted, which were all minor. Once the book came out, he remained curious and claimed, tongue-in-cheek, that he'd never read it. Thankfully, when the book's publication was around the corner and I was cleaning out my project piles, I found the manuscript binder with his handwritten notes. I gleefully presented the evidence to him and had our daughter witness its existence before I threw it out. Nevertheless, when we received the advance reader copies, he sat in his office, feet on his desk, chuckling along as he read the book.

When I asked what was so funny, he said, "This is so interesting! I don't remember any of this."

"What?" I said, "That's your life!"

"Still," he said, "I didn't know this."

This goes to show that:

What you write is your perspective. It will be interesting, even to those who share your life, because their perspective is different.

Aside from my husband, my daughter was the only family member who read the manuscript before it went to print. She is a terrific editor, and I asked her to review the manuscript after I rewrote it. Quite often, she scribbled notes like "That's so Dad!" on the margin. These were great affirmations to me—I had gotten him right! I also received her approval before featuring her in the epilogue. Other family members read the finished book, but they were only minor characters.

My older son found the book "very interesting" and claims the most important thing he learned from it was that you don't have to tell your parents everything. That's definitely an unintended consequence! My younger son will read it at some point, I'm sure, mainly because people keep asking him about it.

Sadly, no one of the older generation is still alive, so I could not get their input or feedback. I was most apprehensive about how my brother and sister would react because they knew the older generation and had their own relationships with them.

That history was also their history.

Thankfully, they both loved the book and were happy to have our family history sorted out. They were gracious enough to recognize that *Jumping Over Shadows* is my version of the family story, and theirs might be different. My brother, who is a graphic designer, helped create a lot of my marketing materials and also provided input on the cover, so to him the book's success is a shared project.

I was also worried about the reaction of my brother-in-law (my husband's brother). There were several reasons for this. First of all, he and my husband had a strained relationship, and a book about the family can exacerbate tensions. Secondly, one never quite knew how he would react. Lastly, I was concerned how he would see my portrayal of his parents.

He himself makes only a cursory appearance in the book, so I didn't feel the need to discuss my project with him beforehand. Nevertheless, the minute the book was available on Amazon, he preordered a copy and proudly told me so via Facebook. Later, he let me know that he had gifted it to several friends, which I took as a good sign. Still, I hadn't heard his opinion.

Then, two months after the book came out, he had a foot amputated (the result of lifelong morbid obesity and ensuing diabetes). I decided to visit him in the hospital in Germany, as I was already crossing the Atlantic to see my older son in Israel. Visiting the sick is always a good deed, but seeing someone who's suffered that kind of calamity was daunting.

In addition, I was walking into a family relationship that was precarious to begin with.

I was in for a pleasant surprise: After talking about his health, we spent most of the visit discussing my book. It was a fruitful conversation, the kind you wish to have with any attentive reader. He commended me on how well I had captured his parents, while also mentioning that he had found it interesting to see his family from my angle. He was astute enough to recognize that my view of his parents would be different than his.

He had only one complaint: Why had I not used his name in the book?

This, thankfully, had been a conscious choice on my part:

- I also hadn't used my brother's, nor my sister's name (nor my children's, for that matter) because I wanted to protect their privacy. This immediately assuaged him—if my siblings had gotten the same treatment, he hadn't been slighted.

- More importantly, not using their names was a technical choice: Since this is a family memoir, the reader has to keep track of a lot of characters. Therefore, minor characters can simply be identified by their relationship to me ("my brother," for example), which makes the text easier to follow. The reader can track who is who, without referring to a family tree.

Talking with my brother-in-law about my book proved again that:

You never know how family will react to being written about, and the way someone reacts is usually indicative of your relationship with them.

I'm glad I visited my brother-in-law for what turned out to be my last visit with him. He passed away in November 2017. I'm thankful for the chance to have talked with him about my book, and I will always be grateful for his attentive reading of my work.

My conversation with him also showed me, once again, that a book is a connector.

Had I not written that book, had I not put it out there, he would not have had the chance to read it, and we would never have had the deep conversation we enjoyed on my last visit. We would not have had the chance to end our connection in this life on a positive, fruitful note.

Prompt:

Confront the uncomfortable! Is there a family member about whose opinion you feel queasy when it comes to your project of writing stories from family history? Take the plunge and share something you wrote with him or her and see if you can have a conversation about it. You might be pleasantly surprised. And even if it ends up being an unpleasant experience, at least you will have the satisfaction that you made the effort.

A Word on Format

As I stated in the beginning, "doing something with" your family history does not mean you have to write a book. There are lots of options to capture snippets of family history in shorter pieces. I mentioned several fine examples throughout this book, and they are collected in the Works Cited chapter for your reference.

The main thing to remember:

Something is better than nothing!

I hope by now you have some good ideas for shorter pieces you could write if you so choose. The very quest of trying to find out the family history could become your storyline.

Quite often, once you have a few shorter pieces, you will find that they circle around a particular topic, and thus they easily form a memoir made of separate but connected stories.

There are so many possibilities to assemble family history stories. Here are some ideas:

- **Photo album with stories**. I've been working on such a book titled "Story of My Things," in which I take photos of a beloved object, such as my grand-mother's wine glasses, and add a short story to go along with the image so that my heirs will know where that item came from and why I cherished it.

- **Ancestry.com book**. I love their format that allows you to supplement a family tree with short stories and photos attached to people's bios.

- **Collection of short memoirs in book format**. It is always a good idea to assemble shorter pieces in a collection, even if it is only for your family's use. I feel this is especially important nowadays, when so much is published online and not necessarily collected in one place of reference. This could also be a page on a blog with links.

- **A book-length memoir**. This is what people tend to bring to mind when they think of memoir: a cohesive, book-length story. You can certainly go for that, but this is not your only option, and it might not be the best option for your project.

Prompt:

Pick one story, object, place, or personality from your family history, and write or create something in a short format you haven't tried before. For example, write a poem if you have never done that. You could, for example, use John Keats' "Ode on a Grecian Urn" as a model and write an ode about a family heirloom. Or you could assemble a photo essay about your childhood home or create a curriculum vitae for one of your ancestors.

Tips on Where to Publish

🖉

I hope I won't disappoint you, but I am not going to offer a list of publications to which you could submit your family history stories. Instead, I urge you to do the following:

Determine the subject you are writing about and look for publications that are interested in that subject area.

This approach offers a greater chance of getting a piece accepted for publication. Here are some examples from my own experience on how this works:

- My story "Thrown Out of the Family Home" appeared in the *Wall Street Journal*. Why? I enjoy reading their Mansion section on Fridays, and I had noticed a call for submissions asking readers to send in stories of beloved homes. It so happened that I thought my story about my odd love for my grandparents' former house in the Czech Republic might fit. It did!

- "Giving Up Christmas" was the first excerpt from my book to be published. I regularly read *Tablet*, which I would wager to say is currently the best Jewish publication in the United States. I noticed that around Christmas time, a Jewish publication like *Tablet* grapples with the issue of what Jews are to do during this all-pervasive holiday season they don't really celebrate. I thought my story about having to give up Christmas as I converted to Judaism would be of interest to them. Sure enough, it was. They particularly liked learning about the Bavarian Christmas customs I had grown up with.

- Seasonal topics always work well, as you can see in my Christmas story. Similarly, I was able to place a story about my wedding, "When Family Boycotts a Wedding," in the *Jewish Journal*, as commercial publications tend to cover weddings in the month of June.

So, for example, if you're writing about something that happened to your family in your neighborhood seventy years ago, a local newspaper might be interested. Or a historical society. Or an anthology covering the history of the area. Check if these publications or institutions accept submissions and, if so, follow their guidelines. Even if they don't, read some of the articles they put out and count how many words they typically have. Then see if you can write your article to fit their style and word count requirements, and simply email it to the editor on the masthead. Your introductory message should be short, simply stating who you are, why you are interested in this subject, and why you think they might be interested. If you have had a similar article published elsewhere that you can link to, do so in order to show off your credentials. If you don't, don't hold back on submitting your story. What have you got to lose?

Sometimes current events will prompt you to write about your family's history, as you can see in Sandi Wisenberg's essay in response to Hurricane Harvey. That was a timely piece, and she did not have much time to write it. You do have to seize the moment when that happens!

Seasonal topics tend to work well, as publications need loads of material on those.

Think about what family history you could write about for Valentine's Day, Easter, Passover, Mother's Day, Father's Day, weddings, Fourth of July, other national holidays, Thanksgiving, Christmas, etc. Anniversaries of historical events are also rife topics—in my case, I can always recycle stories from my book that cover Kristallnacht or Holocaust Remembrance Day. But your story might go along with D-Day, or the attack on Pearl Harbor, or even more recent events such as 9/11. Just keep in mind that print publications need seasonal material about six months in advance, and online publications typically plan a month in advance.

Lastly, look at what you read.

Don't submit your work to publications you don't read yourself. You are more likely to have your work accepted by publications with which you are familiar, simply because the chance is higher that there is a common interest and common style preference.

Prompt:

Make a list of your favorite publications. Then make a list of all the pieces on family history you have written or could write. Would any of them be a fit for one of your favorite publications? If so, whip it into shape and get it out there! If not, see if you can't come up with a few ideas of what you could write for each publication. This will be a work in progress, but you need to have dreams for them to come true!

In Conclusion, Dear Reader

I hope I have given you a few tools and some insight into how to "do something" with your family history. I truly believe it is an important and worthwhile endeavor. I would even venture to say it is the most valuable kind of project in memoir because, even if you have no intention of ever publishing it, you are leaving an account for your family.

I would love to hear how this book has helped you, or whether you have further questions, so please email me at annettegendler@gmail.com, or submit your question to the Advice Column on my blog at annettegendler.com

As a writer there is nothing more precious to me than hearing from a reader.

Many of my ideas for blog posts come from readers' comments and questions, and having a conversation with my readers is great validation of my work.

Finally, **please do me the favor of leaving a review of this book on Amazon**. More than 90 percent of my books sell on Amazon, and each and every review on the site makes them more visible to readers.

Thank you for reading and for connecting with me. I wish you all the best as you embark on writing your own family stories!

Annette

Readings

He Can Walk Because of Me

From Michelle Cox's blog, February 22, 2018

Thomas Bisky was born on June 30, 1910 in Brooklyn, New York, to Stefan Brzezicki and Magda Chmiel. Stefan and Magda were both born in Poland where they met and married. Not much is known about what their life in "the old country" was like, except that Stefan served in the army for a time. At some point, Stefan and Magda managed to immigrate to the United States, where their married name "Brzezicki" was recorded as "Bisky" at their port of entry.

With their new name, the Bisky's settled in Brooklyn, New York, where Thomas was born, and then moved to a farm in Hawley, Pennsylvania, where Stefan worked as not only a farmer, but a coal miner as well. Magda cared for the children, but Thomas can't quite remember how many there were. Besides himself, he remembers Gladys (who legally changed her name to Susan at age seventy), Albert (who went by Frank), Charles and Florence. Thomas's son, Walter, claims that there was also a fourth brother whom no one ever talks about, a "black sheep," who lost contact with the family long ago. And there may have been two more children who died during the flu epidemic, Thomas says, but he isn't sure.

Thomas went to school through the eighth grade and then started working in the mines with his father. He soon tired of this, however, and got a job in construction instead. Jobs were scarce, though, so he moved to New Brighton, Pennsylvania, to find work. When he first got to New Brighton, he stayed in a boarding house and was befriended by another young man, Cal Trenfor, who was staying there. Cal and Thomas became friends, and Cal eventually got around to introducing Thomas to his sister, Ethel. Thomas and Ethel began dating and married soon after. They got an apartment in nearby Elwood City and then bought a house in New Brighton in 1949, where Thomas has since lived all these years.

Thomas got a job at the B&O Steel Mill and worked there for thirty-one years until he retired. He and Ethel had two sons: Thomas, Jr. (Tom) and Walter. Apparently, when Walter was born, he was a breech birth and born with a broken shoulder and crooked feet. Thomas still tears up when telling the story. At the time, Thomas was devastated that his new little son was born "deformed," especially when the doctor said that he would have to go to a special home to live. Thomas refused to send his son away and instead begged the doctor to try to do something himself. Reluctantly, the doctor agreed to try to put special casts and braces on Walter's legs and feet. Shockingly, over time, Walter's legs did indeed straighten out, as much to the doctor's amazement as to everyone else's. Walter was then deemed a "normal" boy by the doctor, who insisted on proudly displaying him to his colleagues. But Thomas also took much pride in the part he played for his son, and often says, "He can walk because of me!"

Thomas apparently did not have many hobbies, except whittling. Also, he and Ethel loved to go dancing on Saturday nights. Both of their boys grew up and moved away: Tom to Virginia Beach and Walter to Chicago. In 1989, Ethel passed away from cancer, and Thomas has been thus living in the house alone, spending his time pottering about and doing a little bit of gardening. Recently, however, both Tom and Walter began to notice that their dad was seeming more and more confused when they would call him on the telephone. Also, he was sounding more and more depressed and was rarely leaving the house. It just so happened that right about this time, Walter's wife, Linda, was looking for a nursing home for her mother and suggested that maybe Walter should arrange for Thomas to be admitted to the same facility.

At first, Thomas was resistant to leaving New Brighton and moving into a nursing home in a different city, but Walter assured him he would visit him daily. Thomas agreed, then, and the house that he and Ethel had lived in for over forty years was sold. Thomas seems to be making a relatively smooth transition to his new home, though he is sometimes confused and forgets where he is. He is quiet and shy and seems nervous most of the time, though he has a wonderful sense of humor when in conversation. He will join in activities, but only when encouraged to several times. His favorite is "Big Band Hour," followed closely by bingo.

Walter has so far kept his promise and visits daily, often bringing his own children or grandchildren along, which Thomas really looks forward to. Despite the fact that they have lived apart for so many years, they seem to share a deep love for each other. When asked about Ethel, Thomas still seems sad but usually catches himself and says, "At least I have Walt."

(Originally written: December 1994)

Reprinted with the author's permission.

The Secret

By Nancy Julien Kopp

My parents eloped on May 31, 1938 in a Chicago suburb. Still the Depression era, but that wasn't the reason Garnet Studham and Gin Julien didn't plan a church wedding. They had no choice since Garnet's mother and two brothers didn't like this man she'd been dating, and they let their feelings be known.

I'd heard the story so many times that the entire elopement seemed as real as watching a movie with my own parents, the main characters.

Gin, whose real name was Alfred, made the arrangements for the wedding with a justice of the peace. On a Tuesday evening, he drove his little coupe to pick up Garnet. She came running down the walk before he could step out of the car. She wore a red linen dress, her short, reddish-brown curls bouncing as she ran.

They drove the few blocks to the JP's home. Gin's hand shook a little when he rang the bell. A woman in a house dress answered and ushered them into the small living room of the bungalow, where her husband waited.

"Sure you want to do this?" he asked, and Gin and Garnet nodded their heads.

No flowers, no cake, no bridesmaid or groomsman. The woman who answered the door would be the legal witness. No music, no guests, no flower girl.

"Alright, let's begin," the JP said. He opened a book to read the words that would bind Gin and Garnet together forever.

A shrill ring interrupted the short service. The witness scurried away to answer the phone while the others waited.

"It's for you," the woman said to her husband, "about the fishing trip tomorrow."

Down went the book and away went the justice of the peace. He had his priorities, and apparently, this quick wedding wasn't high on that list. The wedding couple heard all—where he was going to fish, what time he planned to leave, and who was picking him up. After he boomed, "See you in the morning." The JP returned, mopped his head, retrieved his book, and finished the service. Money changed hands, signatures on a document sealed the marriage, and the newlyweds were ushered out the door with a hurried "congratulations."

"I'm starving," Garnet said as they walked, hand-in-hand, to the little coupe Gin drove.

Gin pecked her on the cheek. "I know just the place."

They went to a favorite bar and grill. Garnet ordered spaghetti and Gin said he wasn't hungry, but he continually tasted bites of the pasta that sat in front of his new wife.

"I thought you weren't hungry," she teased. Weeks later, she learned that he only had enough money in his pocket to pay for one plate.

Before dark, Gin drove his bride to her mother's apartment. Garnet kissed him and then walked slowly to the red-brick building. She spent her wedding night alone in her single bed, afraid to tell her mother or her two brothers what she'd done. And like every other Wednesday morning, she rose long before dawn to work in her mother's small bakery.

Over the next six weeks, Garnet met Gin as many nights as possible for short dates. He urged her to tell her family. The only family he had left were two sisters, both married, but he hadn't told them either. Garnet kept delaying, first by days, then by weeks. Confession would bring undue hurt or might unleash a storm when her brothers found out.

One morning, during a break at the bakery, Garnet sat with her mother at the oil-cloth covered table, sipping a cup of steaming hot tea and nibbling on a sweet roll, fresh from the oven.

Without warning, her mother set her cup down hard and spoke in a voice laced with anger. "You're married, aren't you?" Her mouth was set firmly, no smile to be seen.

Garnet could only nod her head. Words stuck in her throat. How did her mother guess the secret? Garnet's cheeks burned.

Her mother said, "You'd better go live with your husband then." No warmth, no congratulations, no joy.

Garnet cringed from the stinging words. Regret for hurting her mother, relief that the secret had finally come to light, and excitement about joining Gin for good—all these washed over her in one big wave. She packed after work and moved to her husband's tiny studio apartment.

Garnet never did discover how her mother uncovered her secret. Forgiveness was slow, not coming until I was born, exactly two days before their first wedding anniversary. Garnet's two brothers reached across the hospital bed that day to shake Gin's hand while the new grandmother held me close. This time she had a smile for all.

Reprinted with the author's permission. First published in: *Life Story Journal*, April 2019

The Bed

By Diane Hurles

My mother's illness defined my childhood from the time I was seven years old. My older brother, Nick, younger sister, Sue, and I were protected as children. No one ever told us what was really wrong. Cancer was a synonym for death back in the 1960s, so we were told Mom had a "bone disease" and I never thought to question it. There wasn't a moment I didn't believe she'd get well. "When Mom gets better" was our family's mantra, the only timeline we knew.

I learned only when I was in college that Mom had breast cancer. In the shower one morning she had found a lump the size of a pea and soon it had invaded her bones, more specifically her spine. For most of her illness she spent her days in a full-sized hospital bed set up in the middle of our dining room. When I think about Mom, that's how I remember her most—propped up in bed, her dark hair in small pigtails so it wouldn't snarl, with a lime-green wooden bed tray placed in front of her. She ate from that tray, wrote from that tray, and used it to rest her knitting needles and embroidery hoops when she was in the middle of creating a sweater or a cross-stitch sampler.

"Diane, come help me," Mom would yell, and I knew exactly what she wanted me to do: sit next to her bed and hold my arms up in front me so she could drape a new skein of yarn over them and roll it up in a ball for her latest project. I didn't catch on then, but she used those quiet moments, time that usually made me restless, to check in with me, go over my homework, and ask me about my day.

Her bed had a mattress that you could move up and down with a remote control and we used to climb in and "ride" the bed with her. I loved to lie in between the pink-flowered sheets that were Mom's favorites and try out the different mattress positions. Head up, feet down. Head down, feet up. But never both head and feet up at the same time, "the pretzel" we called it, unless Mom happened to be sitting up in her wheelchair and we had the bed to ourselves. I learned early on that, in the cozy confines of her bed, even when I was doing nothing more than holding that skein of yarn, I had to be careful not to get too close, or be too rambunctious, always mindful of how fragile she was. Still, she'd encourage us to join her under the covers on her good days, and I competed with my little sister to see who would get to lie next to her.

One weekend afternoon Mom and I heard a knock at the front door and she asked me to go see who it was. "Are your parents home?" the man on the front stoop asked me. I had never seen him before, but I imagine Mom recognized his voice—or expected his visit—because she called out to me to let him in. I opened the door and watched as he followed her voice into the dining room. Then, as soon as he got there, he stopped. Blatantly. Abruptly. As if his legs had brakes. Oh, I thought, he's never been here before. In front of him was not the china-filled hutch and table and chairs he probably expected, but Mom lying in bed, tucked warmly under the covers, with the pillows around her both supporting and comforting her delicate body. "Don't worry, I'm not contagious," she told him, smiling, trying to put him at ease. "I have a bad back." Within a few minutes Mom charmed him into conversation and his uneasiness waned. Even so, I felt sorry for the man. Sorry he was caught by surprise. I should have told him not to be scared of the bed.

Mom couldn't walk without relying on a walker and a big metal back brace with thick beige straps that looked heavy and uncomfortable. It made her torso look too big for the rest of her body.

"How did I get so wide?" she once remarked to no one in particular while giving herself a once-over in the mirror. A star drum majorette in high school, and former Ottawa County Peach Queen, she noticed in detail how her weakening body was conforming to the illness. She was shorter; her hair was thinner. Her medication made her develop small tufts of facial hair, which I overheard her complain about to Dad. Looking at her in bed, her fragile, bone-thin arms covered by one of the many frumpy bed jackets she received from friends, it was hard for me to imagine her beauty queen days. I felt sad, knowing how anxious she must be to get better and become that person again. Getting better, I thought, would magically transform her body, so cocooned by the frustrations of her illness, into the butterfly I knew she missed so desperately.

Hospital stays became routine for Mom throughout her treatment and, as much as I missed her, I always dreaded visitation days because I wasn't old enough to go up to her room. Hospital rules said you had to be twelve. Most often Dad would bring her down to the lobby in a wheelchair where we were waiting. But sometimes we would beat the system and the nurses, oozing with compassion for two scared young girls, would sneak Sue and me up the back stairwell, reassuring us all the way that it was OK.

"Your mom's been talking about you coming all morning," they'd say.

Still, it felt awkward and wrong. I'm sure I tried to hop in bed for a ride once we got up to her room, probably more than once, but quickly learned their compassion had limits.

"Careful, honey. Your mom's had a rough morning," the nurse would warn protectively, no doubt referring to the bouts of nausea that often accompanied the mega doses of medicine she received in the hospital.

"Don't listen to them," Mom would respond with a laugh.

But, embarrassed, I'd shrug it off with a quick, "That's OK," and lean against the wall, or stand by the door, for the rest of the visit, anxious to get going.

When she was home, Mom was often groggy from pain medication and there were many times when I'd settle in next to her on the bed to watch television, only to have her fall asleep during the good parts. It frustrated me, but I still cherished those TV times when we'd watch *The King Family* or *Lawrence Welk* on a small black and white set that was suspended from the ceiling so she could see the screen comfortably from the bed. I don't remember watching much drama, or even comedy for that matter, just happy, upbeat singers. There was a comfort to the music that matched the comfort of the bed. Stretched out in my pajamas next to Mom, the pillows fluffed up, while watching those impossibly perky singers, singing wholesome songs with lipstick-bright smiles on their faces gave me some of the greatest sense of security I remember having as a child. For an hour or two I was living in their world, where everything was perfect, thinking ahead to the day when my world would be perfect too.

Everything will be OK, those singers were telling me. And I believed them.

Most times, though, away from the TV and the bedcovers, I felt anything but secure. With Mom's sickness came the constant concern and sympathy of others, pity that filled me with an almost tangible self-consciousness, as if I were walking around with a big asterisk over my head.

*She's different.

*Poor thing.

*Be nice.

I was embarrassed because my family was different. I was uncomfortable because people singled us out. All I really wanted to feel was normal. More than anything, I wanted to feel normal.

"Normal" to me back then meant being able to do family things on the spur of the moment. It meant blending in at school. And it meant having the kind of house my friends had with new furniture and plush carpet. A house kept neat enough for us to invite people over on a whim. Especially one that didn't have a bed in the dining room. But the closest I remember we ever got to new furniture after Mom became sick was a dark green slipcover with gold fringe for the living room couch, so when she and Dad announced they wanted to redecorate the upstairs bedroom Sue and I shared as a special gift, I was over the moon.

The project quickly became an event. My grandmother drove from Ohio to help us pore over wallpaper samples, paint swatches and furniture catalogs. Mom's bed became our palette as we plopped big bulky sample books all around her, matching colors and patterns, eventually choosing a wallpaper dizzy with red and pink roses. We furnished it with all-white furniture trimmed in gold. It took several weeks, but once the room was finally finished I sat on my new bed with its new sheets and matching bedspread, totally absorbed in happiness, wondering if I could have a slumber party to show it off to my friends. I felt proud—and normal.

Although she shared our excitement, Mom couldn't enjoy our decorating project as enthusiastically as we did. Too weak to go upstairs to see the bedroom transformation for herself, she had to be content with the pictures Dad took to show her what the finished room looked like.

With her illness so all consuming, staying connected to us was a priority for Mom, so much so, that she once wrote about the importance of communicating with your children for a mother-daughter banquet at our church. The banquet was an annual event, a celebration of all of the women in the church, with the men volunteering to cook and serve dinner. I have vague memories of attending an earlier banquet with Mom when we first moved to Detroit, but this time she was too ill to go, so Mrs. Lang, our pastor's wife, invited Sue and me to go with her. If only by proxy, Mom was determined to have a presence there, and composed the special message which she asked Mrs. Lang to read aloud during the program.

"Take time out of your too-busy day to truly look at your children and honestly listen to them," Mom wrote to the audience. "I have lots of time now to do just this and I've learned so much more about my children than ever before. Knitting and embroidery keep my hands and mind busy, but the best part of my day is when school is out and the door flies open and the kids yell, 'Mom, I'm home!' Then flop on my bed with all their news of the day."

I wish I could remember the last time I flopped on her bed with news, good or bad. I wish I could remember the sound of her voice and the touch of her hand during those moments when she followed her own advice and truly looked at me. I lost those details long ago. But the lessons that resonated from all of the pillow talks we shared have stayed with me throughout my adolescence and adulthood, resonating most deeply when I became a mother myself: Be present for those you love. Never give up hope. Value the time you're given.

"Despite our adversities we still live a happy, hectic life," Mom wrote from her bed for that mother-daughter banquet, "and each day I treasure the moments I'm alive."

Mom died just months after she composed those words, five years after first discovering her cancer. Despite what our family had been through, I was caught by surprise, relentlessly clinging to my belief that she'd get well until I had no choice but to let go.

I don't think it took us long to transform the house. As I remember it, one morning I left for school and the bed was still there in its usual place, the mattress empty and stripped of linens, and when I came home that afternoon the small table and chairs from the kitchen had taken its place. The room had been dusted and vacuumed, the curtains were fresh from the dryer, and a small centerpiece sat on the table. It was back to being just as intended—The Dining Room— as if it had never had another purpose. It took us a long time to use it that way; for a full year after Mom's death, we all but ignored that table, preferring to eat our dinner on trays in front of the TV in a darkened living room. Just like our house, we were in transition.

We couldn't see beyond the bed.

Reprinted with the author's permission. First published in *Wisdom Has a Voice: Every Daughter's Memories of Mother*, Kate Farrell (ed.), Unlimited Publishing LLC, 2011

Queen of the Night

(excerpt from *Jumping Over Shadows* by Annette Gendler)

Until his own marriage in 1932, my grandfather was the bachelor in the family, and thus he had the time to play a prominent role in the lives of his niece and nephew, Herta and Ludwig. He became der Onkel, the Uncle. Herta had wonderful memories of the Uncle and the stories he used to tell. When he had wrapped up his work as principal of the girls' middle school and editor of the *Freie Schulzeitung*, the Free School Paper, he would be up late at night in the apartment on Tuchplatz, dreaming up a story to tell Herta and Ludwig the following weekend.

He also grew cacti in the white light of the turret room overlooking Tuchplatz. One summer night after Herta and Ludwig had already been tucked into bed, their doorbell rang. Shortly thereafter, Resi came into their room and said, "Come on, you two, get dressed again. The Uncle wants us to come over. He has something special to show us."

Herta and Ludwig got ready fast. Going out again after they had already been sent to bed was exciting and most unusual.

The whole family hurried along the streets. The sun had just set. Tuchplatz was busy with people and streetcars and open restaurants. They clattered up the stairs to the Uncle's apartment, Herta's clogs booming through the stairwell.

"Well, there you are." The Uncle was waiting by the door. "Come in, come in. I have something special to show you."

He led them, tiptoeing, almost as if afraid to disturb someone, into the living room and on into the turret's alcove.

"Look, the Queen of the Night is about to open its blossom."

They bent over a cactus sitting on the windowsill. Its long, flat leaves, their edges scalloped, flopped out of a ceramic pot. One of those leaves had a blossom hanging off its side. It looked as if the cactus were holding out a little cup of white fur. The Uncle crouched down to be at eye level with the children and the plant.

"Do you know what's so special about this?" he asked.

They shook their heads.

"The Queen of the Night opens its blossom only once, at night. By midnight it is in full bloom, and by morning it is gone. And it smells wonderful."

Indeed, the Queen of the Night unfolded its white cup into a blossom that reminded Herta of a daisy, only smaller and bushier. Some of its petals hung down like a fringy skirt.

They all sat about in the Stube, nibbling on cookies and sipping tea. Every few minutes, someone checked on the Queen of the Night. The Uncle had his camera out and moved it this way and that on the tripod, the lens pointed toward the blossom.

"No one near it, please," he admonished them. "I need a lot of exposure; I don't want to use a flash."

Resi sniffed the air. "Hmm, I can already smell it."

The kids insisted on staying until midnight even though they were feeling drowsy. At midnight, the blossom was wide open and an intensely haunting scent filled the room. Herta wasn't sure she liked it.

"Wonderful, this scent," Resi kept saying. "Simply extraordinary."

"I'm not so sure," Guido said. "It's a bit too intense, don't you think?"

The adults went back and forth about the scent, and Herta and Ludwig ate more cookies. Eventually their parents hurried them back home, but not before promising to return the next day to check on the cactus. The following evening, Herta could hardly believe that the white blossom had wilted and was hanging off the cactus's side, limp and brown.

This nocturnal excursion must have happened in 1930 or 1931, when Herta was old enough to remember; when my grandfather was still a bachelor and my grandmother wasn't around yet to steer him toward more practical pursuits; when he could afford to indulge in the tending of cacti and in the giddy joy over a rare blossom. A time when he could make Resi and Guido, Ludwig and Herta rush along the city streets on a warm summer night to climb up to the turret room to watch a white blossom spread open and release its bittersweet fragrance.

Works Cited

Short Memoirs:

Gendler, Annette. "Giving Up Christmas as a Convert to Judaism." *Tablet*. December 19, 2012.

Gendler, Annette. "House Call: 'Thrown Out' of the Family Home." *The Wall Street Journal*. July 5, 2013.

Gendler, Annette. "The Tractor." *Thread*. May 31, 2016.

Gendler, Annette. "When Family Boycotts a Wedding." *Jewish Journal*. July 5, 2017.

McClanahan, Rebecca. "My Father's Cadillac." *New and Selected Poems*. New York: Iris Press, 2007.

Palmer, Larry. "Urshel—The Beautiful Black Sheep." *Blackbird*. Spring 2016.

Wigoda, Susan. "Wednesdays and Sundays." *Intima, A Journal of Narrative Medicine*. Spring 2014.

Wisenberg, Sandi. "After Harvey, A Requiem for Jewish Houston." *Tablet*. September 1, 2017.

Book-length Memoirs:

Baker, Russell. *Growing Up*. New York: Berkeley, 1992.

Doty, Mark. *Firebird*. New York: Harper, 2000.

Douglas, Ellen. *Truth: Four Stories I am Finally Old Enough to Tell*. New York: Algonquin Books, 1998.

Durrell, Gerald. *My Family and Other Animals*. New York: Penguin, 2004.

Ginzburg, Natalia. *The Things We Used to Say*. New York: Arcade Publishing, 1999.

Gornick, Vivian. *Fierce Attachments*. New York: Macmillan, 2005.

Jordan, Teresa. *Riding the White Horse Home: A Western Family Album*. New York: Penguin Random House, 1994.

Karr, Mary. *Cherry*. New York: Penguin, 2001.

Karr, Mary. *Lit: A Memoir*. New York: Harper, 2010.

Karr, Mary. *The Liars' Club*. New York: Penguin, 1995.

Mackall, Joe. *The Last Street Before Cleveland*. Lincoln: University of Nebraska Press, 2014.

McClanahan, Rebecca. *The Tribal Knot*. Bloomington: Indiana University Press, 2013.

McCourt, Frank. *Angela's Ashes*. New York: Scribner, 1999.

De Waal, Edmund. *The Hare with Amber Eyes*. UK: Picador, 2011.

Simpson, Eileen. *Orphans: Real and Imaginary*. New York: Grove Press, 1987.

Simpson, Eileen. *Poets in Their Youth: A Memoir*. New York: Farrar, Strauss and Giroux, 2014.

Simpson, Eileen. *Reversals: A Personal Account of Victory over Dyslexia*. New York: Farrar, Strauss and Giroux, 1998.

Steinberg, Michael. *Still Pitching*. East Lansing: Michigan State University Press, 2003.

Wolff, Tobias. *This Boy's Life*. New York: Grove Press, 2000.

How-to and Reference:

Barrington, Judith. *Writing the Memoir*. Portland: Eight Mountain Press, 2002.

Doty, Mark. "Return to Sender: Memory, Betrayal, and Memoir." *The Writer's Chronicle*. AWP. October/November 2005.

Hirsch, Marianne. *The Generation of Post Memory*. New York: Columbia University Press, 2012.

McKee, Robert. *Story*. New York: Harper Collins, 2010.

Root, Roberta Brown. "An Interview of Susan Cheever." *The Writer's Chronicle*. AWP. May/Summer 2005.

Stern, Jerome. *Making Shapely Fiction*. New York: W.W. Norton & Company, 1991.

Wolynn, Mark. *It Didn't Start With You*. New York: Penguin, 2017.

Further Reading

Following is a list of memoirs of family history done particularly well. Some of these books I have already mentioned; others I didn't. I offer you this list because the best way to learn is to read how others did what you are trying to do. While these books are all concerned with family history, each author went about it differently, and that is the best inspiration ever. I hope you find at least one example you could mirror!

Abu-Jaber, Diana. *The Language of Baklava.* New York: Anchor, 2006.

Adorjan, Johanna. *An Exclusive Love.* New York: W. W. Norton & Company, 2012.

Balakian, Peter. *Black Dog of Fate.* New York: Basic Books, 2009.

Brown, Nickole. *Fanny Says.* Rochester, NY: BOA Editions Ltd, 2015.

Danticat, Edwidge. *Brother, I'm Dying.* New York: Vintage, 2008.

De Waal, Edmund. *The Hare with Amber Eyes.* UK: Picador, 2011.

Ginzburg, Natalia. *The Things We Used to Say.* New York: Arcade Publishing, 1999.

Huang, Wenguang. *The Little Red Guard.* New York: Riverhead Books, 2013.

McClanahan, Rebecca. *The Tribal Knot.* Bloomington: Indiana University Press, 2013.

Ondaatje, Michael. *Running in the Family.* New York: Vintage, 1993.

Wildman, Sarah. *Paper Love.* New York: Riverhead Books, 2015.

Acknowledgments

A big thank you to all my readers and workshop participants who egged me on to create a book based on my workshop, "Shaping Family History into Compelling Stories." Without their questions and suggestions, it would not have occurred to me to write this book.

Thank you, as always, to my family for giving me the space and peace to write, and to all my beta readers and my advance team for their time, diligence, and ever-so-helpful suggestions.

A version of "Writing About Others" appeared in the *Washington Independent Review of Books*, October 3, 2013.

A version of "Filling in the Blanks of My Jewish Family History" appeared on *Rivka's Yiddish*, May 21, 2017.

About the Author

Annette Gendler is the author of *Jumping Over Shadows*, the memoir of a German-Jewish love that overcame the legacy of the Holocaust.

Her work has appeared in the *Wall Street Journal*, *Tablet Magazine*, *Bella Grace*, and *Kveller*, among others. She has been teaching memoir writing at StoryStudio Chicago since 2006 and also served as the writer-in-residence at the Hemingway Birthplace Home in Oak Park, Illinois. She holds an MFA in Creative Writing from Queens University of Charlotte and lives in Chicago with her husband and three children.

Her popular workshop Shaping Family History into Compelling Stories was the basis for this book. She regularly offers it at StoryStudio Chicago but has also taken it on the road to Boston, Jerusalem, and the Festival of Faith and Writing.